This book
belongs to
Billi Rondersin
I was bought
in Cabridge
o June 10th
1987

THE HOME UNIVERSITY LIBRARY
OF MODERN KNOWLEDGE

135

A HISTORY OF ENGLAND
1815-1939

A History of England
1815–1939

Sir JAMES BUTLER

Second Edition

LONDON
OXFORD UNIVERSITY PRESS
NEW YORK   TORONTO
1960

Oxford University Press, Amen House, London E.C.4

GLASGOW NEW YORK TORONTO MELBOURNE WELLINGTON
BOMBAY CALCUTTA MADRAS KARACHI KUALA LUMPUR
CAPE TOWN IBADAN NAIROBI ACCRA

First published in 1928 *and reprinted in* 1932, 1936, 1942,
1945 *and* 1949
Second edition 1960

PRINTED IN GREAT BRITAIN

CONTENTS

NOTE TO SECOND EDITION

The present re-issue of this little book contains a new chapter on the years 1919–1939; the bibliography has also been revised. I have to thank Dr. W. J. Macpherson for calling my attention to some recent works, and I wish to repeat my previous acknowledgements to the late Professor Graham Wallas and Mr. D. A. Winstanley and to Lord McNair, Professor T. H. Marshall and my brother, Sir Nevile Butler.

J. R. M. B.

January 1959

HISTORY OF ENGLAND, 1815—1939

CHAPTER I

THE AFTERMATH OF WAR

THE century spanning the interval between the Great War of 1914 to 1918 and the last great war before it must always rank among the cardinal periods of English history. It changed the face and outlook of England as no previous century had changed them. Wide expanses of green country were turned into towns and suburbs, and hard roads and railways seamed the surface of the land. The numbers of the population rose beyond all precedent, and the northern districts became, for the first time, the most thickly inhabited. Wealth was prodigiously increased : rich men, using capital on a scale that seemed colossal, applied and exploited the new scientific knowledge for their own gain and to the general convenience. New mechanical processes led to a specialization of labour which transformed the conditions of the people's work and leisure; trains, bicycles, and motor-cars gave them a mobility undreamed of before; cheap education, cheap newspapers, and a cheap post broke down the barriers that isolated their minds. Natural science suggested entirely new ways of regarding the universe and man, and introduced scientific method into other spheres of thought. Religion, though encouraged by science to compromise with materialism, yet thanks to science formed less anthropomorphic conceptions of deity. In literature, the torch of English poetry was carried on and the novel reached its highest development as an interpreter of the human heart. In politics, the machinery of government was made far more elaborate and efficient than ever before, while the gathering of working men into closely populated areas made combination possible among them, so that political power passed from a landed and mercantile aristocracy to the majority of the male population organized in national parties. Overseas, vigorous communities of white settlers won self-government within the British State, and new empires were acquired in Asia, central Africa and the South Seas.

The history of England in this period was profoundly affected by three movements which began in the previous century, the one religious, the one economic, and the third political. The religious revival connected with the names of Wesley and Whitefield was the least spectacular of the three, but it would be wrong to ignore the importance of the impulse which gave a new well-spring of thought and action to so many thousands of men and women in Wales and England, enabling them to endure without despair the hardships of an age of transition. The complex of changes in agriculture, industry and commerce known as the Industrial Revolution radically altered the outward circumstances of men's lives and their views of society and their own place in it. The French Revolution, destroying as in a night the ancient structure of society and ancient ideas of human values, had probably less effect in England than either of the other two movements ; but it was more sudden, and so more clearly marked the beginning of a new era, and it set loose intellectual forces of immense attractive and repulsive power. It is moreover inseparably connected in history with the war which for nearly the quarter of a century cut England off from the Continent and intensified the more baneful effects of the revolution in industry.

Certainly on the political side, and probably from a wider point of view, the period from Waterloo to Mons falls naturally into two equal halves between which the prosperous sixties form the watershed. In home politics the end of the Palmerstonian epoch and the enfranchisement of the town worker coincided with the emergence of new ideas as to the sphere and function of the State. Foreign policy no less assumed a new colour in the shadow of the rising power of Prussia and the spectacle of terrific wars on both sides of the Atlantic. It will be convenient to follow this division in the structure of this short survey, but, as the war of 1914 forms an epilogue to the century, so at the beginning the years immediately following the Napoleonic war require treatment as a separate episode.

The Britain of 1815 presents strangely different aspects according to the point of view of the observer. To the student of world politics, she towered supreme in wealth and strength and prestige. She had indeed saved herself by her exertions and Europe by her example. In the darkest hour her courage had never quailed. Thanks to her incomparable navy, no foreign foe had marched through the streets of London, and while her allies had been losing provinces she had added to her empire Malta, Ceylon and the Cape. For ten years her command of the sea had been unchallenged, and her fleets were now superior to those of the rest of Europe combined. If some of her industries had suffered cruelly from the war, others had reaped huge profits, and it was her subsidies that had strengthened her allies to maintain the almost hopeless combat. In the final struggle with Napoleon, her armies in Spain and Flanders had played a great part and her diplomacy a greater. It was a British statesman, Castlereagh, whose patience and moderation had built up and held together the last, and the only successful, alliance against France, and a British general, Wellington, who commanded the allied armies now occupying French soil. And in one notable instance Britain had given a moral lead to the nations : having abolished the slave trade herself, she fought hard and successfully for its abolition in the territories of other States.

Nor, to the outward view, was the prospect at home less dazzling. Alone in western Europe the ark of the British constitution had weathered the revolutionary deluge. The old mad king was the idol of his people ; if the son who reigned in his place had a different reputation, his Court was the apex, if not the centre, of an aristocracy proverbial for its brilliance. Those who doubted the claims of the Prince Regent to be the first gentleman in Europe might on other grounds admit those of the Duke of Wellington. Outside the fashionable circle, landlords and farmers, bankers and investors, had been enjoying amazing prosperity, and vast fortunes had been made in the adventurous fields of the new industry. In Continental eyes every Englishman was a lord and a millionaire, and he expected to be treated as such when he deigned to travel abroad.

But behind this imposing façade the fabric of society showed deep rifts and much of it was rotten. Among the ruling class standards of public and private morality were usually low. Positions in Church and State went by favour, and were often treated as sinecures. Many of the parish clergy took a narrow view of their duties, and some rarely visited their flocks. There was an exaggerated regard for vested interests, which shared the veneration attaching to property. Respect for property prevented the reform of countless abuses and disgraced the criminal code with ferocious punishments. Rich men were allowed to protect their woods with spring guns, and a thief could be sentenced to death or transportation. Orators might boast that England was a free country and that there was one law for all; but freedom means little to a starving man, and a law which mainly concerned itself with the defence of property could not look the same to those who had great possessions as to those who had none. Even when the law was on the poor man's side he might lack the money to move its cumbrous wheels.

Unfortunately the recent changes in agriculture and industry had made the livelihood of the poor more insecure than ever. In the country the self-supporting village community, with its easy-going but uneconomic methods, was declining, and the condition of thousands of labourers was pitiable. In the teeming towns, where the smoke of factory and forge was already fouling the air, there was growing up an ill-fed and over-worked proletariat, unorganized and uneducated, protected against neither the caprice of their masters nor the uncertainties of trade. For the opinion of the age condemned State interference on principle, and left the forces of the new industrialism to sweep unchecked on their momentous course.

The new conditions tended to a weakening of sympathy between the classes. Hitherto the landed aristocracy had understood the villagers, their immemorial neighbours, and some part of them had been in alliance with the traders of the towns. Now things were different. England was still predominantly rural, but the changes of the last forty years had brought an end to many old personal relations. In the towns there was less tradition of friendship. Few among the gentry, few among the rich middle class, understood the feelings of the grimy slum-dwellers eking out a squalid life strange even to themselves. Understanding little and therefore fearing much, the ruling class regarded the poor almost as a subject race whose poverty and ignorance might prompt, as in France, to violence ; yet they were loath to allow them the leisure for learning or the right of combining to better their condition.

These deepset evils were aggravated by temporary grievances incidental to the change from war to peace conditions and to the whims of the English climate. The government was totally incapable of dealing with the crisis ; perhaps no government would have been capable, but Lord Liverpool's Tory Cabinet and House of Commons between them went out of their way to make things worse. Consequently the peace was followed by six terrible years of misery and hatred, famine, bloodshed and scandal ; an epoch of suppressed civil war. Then almost suddenly the tension relaxed ; the solid strength and constructive genius of the nation began to assert themselves, and from the early twenties things began to improve, slowly and intermittently at first, but with gathering momentum as the century neared its middle. As it happens, the bad years coincided with an episode of special interest in foreign relations, marked by the attempt of Castlereagh, the Foreign Secretary, to work for the maintenance of peace in intimate collaboration with the late European allies. As these States were controlled by autocrats determined to use the new diplomatic harmony for the purpose of regulating the internal concerns of other nations, Castlereagh's policy became associated in English opinion with the cause of European reaction and increased the hostility to the government; his critics' suspicions would have been allayed had he allowed them to know that he was in fact opposing with all his might these designs of the Holy Alliance.

The troops came home from France and Flanders to find food dear, taxes high, wages in many trades low, and employment scarce. The longed-for day had come, but conditions seemed worse than ever. An England which hardly remembered itself at peace was called upon to adapt its ways and institutions, without the stimulus of war, to economic conditions the like of which the world had never seen. Ancient landmarks had been swept away, and the wisdom of bygone ages gave no help.

Among the chief of the special circumstances which embittered these years was the mad fluctuation in the price of wheat. In August 1813 the quarter had stood at 112*s.*; then it had begun to fall, and in January 1816 was down to 52*s.* 6*d.* In June it rose to 117*s.* Dismayed at the thought of losing the war prices they had learnt to live up to, the landowners in parliament passed a Corn law in 1815 prohibiting the importation of wheat when the price was under 80*s.* This measure failed to save them from a period of acute depression, but it sufficed to infuriate the industrial classes and the poor of town and country alike, who complained that parliament was set on making the war stringency perpetual. A rise of the poor-rate from nearly £5,500,000 in 1815 to nearly £8,000,000 in 1818 showed how large a dole was thought necessary to prevent starvation.

Apart from the price of food, the industrial population of the towns had their own woes. The new lords of business were exploring an uncharted sea; they produced for speculative markets, and often their guesses were faulty; the credit system was inadequate; there were violent fluctuations of prosperity, and of course the poor suffered most. The end of the war meant a sudden curtailment of government orders in the clothing trade and the iron and steel trades. Manufacturers had not foreseen that continental customers would be too poor to buy British products; both exports and imports actually fell.   Trade depression brought almost universal cuts in wages and catastrophic unemployment, to which the discharge of hundreds and thousands of soldiers and sailors contributed.

The riots which had protested against the passing of the Corn bill were justified.   In 1816 sheer hunger led to violent outbreaks in some districts and a general outcry against existing conditions.   Besides numerous strikes there were rioting and arson in East Anglia and frame-breaking in the lace districts, to atone for which twelve men were executed.   In January 1817 an attempt was made on the life of the Regent ; in March a pilgrimage of wretchedly paid weavers marching from Manchester to present a petition was dispersed by troops ; in the summer two futile outbreaks were easily suppressed. Two hangings and eleven transportations for life were the result.

Far more important than these vain demonstrations was the awakening of political interest among the working classes.   The long dormant demand for a reform of parliament and a democratic suffrage was revived by a band of demagogues of whom the greatest was William Cobbett.   Public meetings were held, organizations were formed, and Cobbett's *Political Register,* the pioneer of Radical journalism, reached a

circulation of between forty and fifty thousand.
Cobbett urged his readers to concentrate on
parliamentary reform. Parliament was responsible for corrupt government, high taxes,
inflated prices. The working class must capture it and restore the golden age England had
enjoyed before she was ruined by manufacturers,
economists, profiteers and potatoes. In their
attacks on the political order and their demand
for democratic reform the demagogues found
allies in the disciples of Jeremy Bentham.
Otherwise Bentham and Cobbett were as unlike
as two men could be, Cobbett's racy English,
reckless denunciations and cheery out-of-doors
bluster contrasting oddly with the uncouth
logical formulæ of the gentle old lawyer-philo-
sopher who in " the greatest happiness of the
greatest number " had found the talisman of
political improvement.

Now to members of parliament, and people
over forty generally, the proceedings of 1816-17
were almost bound to suggest the French Revolution. It was not twenty-five years since the
execution of Louis XVI and the September
Massacres. These horrors had developed from
perfectly innocent-seeming beginnings. Accordingly during the war every critic of the government had been reputed a Jacobin ; in Scotland,
men had been sent to Botany Bay for advocat-

ing reform of parliament. Now the war was over, but it was only just over, and the obsession remained. Whatever benefits the French Revolution may have brought to Continental politics and to English literature, in English politics its influence was wholly pernicious. For at least a generation it soured the milk of English kindness and made democracy a bugbear. In the face of rioting, destruction of property, and indignation meetings, Lord Liverpool's government, served by no impartial information and no reliable police, suspended the Habeas Corpus Act and strengthened the law against seditious assemblies. Sidmouth, the Home Secretary, the Addington of grander days, urged county authorities to enrol special constables, hold the Yeomanry ready, and be instant in making arrests ; he went further, and lower, and enrolled spies, who were not ashamed to instigate crime and then inform against their dupes. Public meetings soon became impossible ; even the Cambridge Union Society suspended its debates. The government had won, and owing partly to a good harvest the year 1818 was quiet.

But, though business improved, wages were not raised, and the boom in certain trades, which followed on the slump, led in its turn to a crisis. There were strikes in the north at the end of the year, and in 1819 the storm of discontent broke out afresh, with more angry meetings, more political societies among working men, and more demands for reform of parliament. A huge gathering at Birmingham chose itself a parliamentary representative in defiance of the law; a huge and peaceable gathering at Manchester was clumsily broken up by the Yeomanry, eleven of the unarmed crowd being killed and several hundreds wounded. This "Peterloo Massacre" caused widespread indignation, and the movement grew. The government promptly increased the army by 10,000 recruits and summoned parliament to meet in November to pass a new batch of repressive laws, some temporary and some permanent. The right of bearing arms, the right of public meeting, and the freedom of the Press were drastically curtailed in spite of an unusually vigorous parliamentary opposition. The year 1819 had added Peterloo, the Six Acts, and the names of Liberal and Radical to the political vocabulary.

Francis Place, a good judge, believed the country to be on the verge of civil war, and the new year and the new reign—for George III died in January 1820—opened under the gloomiest auguries. A plot to assassinate the entire Cabinet was detected; the revolution in Spain gave hope to the reformers, and there were several abortive outbreaks. But then suddenly a sorry personal incident, which well illustrates the caprice of history, diverted the course of events. The accession of George IV brought to a head his feud with his wife. No matrimonial affairs had played such a part in English history since the days of Henry VIII and his daughters. Queen Caroline's rights and wrongs and the characters of the disreputable pair became the topic of debate in every circle from the House of Lords downwards. The Opposition, in and out of parliament, exploited the people's hatred of the husband and sympathy for the wife. The monarchy has never sunk so low in the nation's respect, but the immediate result was to tide over the social danger. By the time the unsavoury excitement subsided, prices had fallen, food was cheaper, and trade had improved. The " Radical War " had misfired. Yet the prestige of the Ministry had been rudely shaken, and it seemed that the ensuing " truce between parliament and the people " must shortly lead to political reforms. Peel and Canning, who succeeded to the Home and Foreign secretaryships, and Huskisson, who became President of the Board of Trade, were all enlightened Tories, in sympathy with the spirit of the age ; they did in fact inaugurate a new epoch of liberal government in which prosperity at length by slow degrees returned to the country and in which the memory of the terrible years before it faded gradually away like the memory of a bad dream. To us that memory is preserved by the passionate denunciations of Shelley and Byron, the one so naïve and the other so cynical a hater of oppression. But, lest we lose proportion, let us remember that in these years the comfortable novels of Scott and Jane Austen were first seeing the light, and that the year which produced Peterloo produced also the Odes to a Nightingale and on a Grecian Urn.

CHAPTER II

THE GROWTH OF WEALTH

WE cannot tell what aspect of nineteenth century England will seem most remarkable to future historians. To contemporary observers it was her economic aspect. Notable for her navy, notable for her constitution, she impressed them chiefly as the pioneer of the new industrial civilization, as the land of economic adventure whose capitalists had won fabulous riches for themselves and her. In 1815 the industrial revolution had passed through two-thirds of its first phase, the phase before the railways, and the tide of change was still flowing strong and fast. The main general effects had begun to define themselves, but the nature, occasion, and rate of transformation differed widely in different industries. In many the old and the new conditions existed side by side for years, and it was not till after the great trade depression of 1837–42 that the victory of the new was apparent.

The rapid increase of population was of course

both an effect and a cause of the increase of wealth. The inhabitants of Great Britain numbered just over 14 millions in 1821 ; the figure had been 10½ millions in 1801, and was to be 26 millions in 1871. In the ten years before 1821 it was rising at a faster rate than ever before or since. Meanwhile the centre of gravity was shifting from the country to the towns, and huge urban populations were collecting in the north-west of England, in South Wales and between the firths of Forth and Clyde. In Ireland, where the increase was nearly twice as rapid as in England during the main period of the industrial revolution, the population numbered nearly 7 millions in 1821 ; it reached over 8 millions in 1841, but by 1871 had sunk to less than 5½ millions. From the beginning of the century the flow of Irish immigrants into the western districts of Great Britain was an important factor in the supply of unskilled labour. From the twenties onwards, however, there was a considerable stream of emigration to North America from all the three kingdoms.

The premier British industry in 1821, alike in numbers and in prestige, was agriculture. During the war the difficulty of feeding the swelling numbers of the beleaguered island and the prospect of monopoly prices encouraged agriculturists to bring every possible rood of land into cultivation. The national need tended to transform the villages from self-sufficient communities into factories for producing food, and tradition gave way to efficiency. Squires and farmers on long leases waxed fat on high rents and high prices. Loath to see their new affluence forsake them when peace came, the country gentry passed the Corn Act of 1815. But although up till 1840 England imported less than one-fifteenth of her wheat, agriculture suffered a severe depression for a generation. The yield of British wheat was increased by $5\frac{1}{2}$ million quarters, but the Corn laws did not prevent wild fluctuations of price according to the chances of the harvest. Meanwhile the poor-rate was becoming an intolerable burden. From the mid-thirties things became easier : the Poor Law was reformed, roads were improved, tithes were commuted, agricultural knowledge became diffused. Farmers learnt to drain clay soils, to use artificial manures, to buy fodder for their stock, and to use implements that saved time and labour. After 1853, despite the repeal of the Corn laws, agriculture enjoyed its golden age, sharing in the general rise of prices. For twenty years yet Britain depended mainly on her own produce ; rents and profits rose, and a high standard of farming spread widely. Though it no longer provided the bulk of the nation's wealth, land remained the most dignified and desirable form of property, and to acquire it was to rise in the social scale.

Among the new sources of wealth the cotton trade was far the most spectacular. Of only secondary importance before the end of the eighteenth century, mechanical inventions and the judicious exploitation of the geographical advantages of the west coast raised it to the front rank in the course of two generations. It was the type of the new economic order. Raw cotton from America was spun and woven in Lancashire to clothe the inhabitants not of the British Isles only but of the continent of Europe, both Americas, and even India, the ancient home of the craft. It was spun, in 1815, largely by steam-driven machinery in mills or factories owned by capitalists and employing the labour of hundreds of men, women, and children ; the yarn was woven as yet principally on hand-looms in the workers' homes, but there were 14,000 power-looms at work in 1820, and by 1833 as many as 100,000—perhaps half the number of hand-looms. One mechanical improvement followed another, and the amount of raw cotton imported rose from 82 million pounds in 1815 to over 1,000 million in 1860.

The wool trade was as old in prestige as its rival, the cotton industry, was new. In it a similar transformation took place, but much more slowly; there were longer traditions to break down. Nevertheless power spinning was driving out hand spinning in the first thirty years of the century, and the spinning of wool was ceasing to be a by-employment. In weaving the old methods held their ground longer, and did not give place to the factory till the fifties. By then the industry was concentrated in the West Riding of Yorkshire. At the same time it was coming to depend on imported wool. As late as 1850 the home yield of wool far exceeded the imports; by 1870 the proportion was more than reversed, imports having risen to 266 million pounds. Australia, New Zealand and the Cape had then become the chief sources of supply.

A parallel development had been taking place in metallurgy. The iron trade, like the cloth trade, had thriven on government orders during the war, and suffered severely when they ceased. But its future was assured by the successive great inventions, which were to make the new era an iron age. The annual output rose from 150,000 tons in 1800 to nearly 1,400,000 tons in 1840; iron was then wanted for railways and would soon be wanted for steamships. Meanwhile the industry of mechanical engineering had established itself. The early machines in the textile trades had been of wood, driven first by hand and then by water power; later, as steam came into use, there was a demand for iron engines, made individually by hand. After 1820 came the production of machine tools—machines to turn out other machines that should be accurate and uniform as well as durable—such as Nasmyth's steam-hammer in 1839. In the forties and fifties marine engineering became an important industry by itself. By this time the legal restrictions on the export of machinery had been removed, partially in 1825 and fully in 1843; the value of the machinery exported rose from under a million sterling in 1845 to over 5 millions in 1865, when the world was demanding from England the implements of the new civilization.

All these developments depended on coal, the upstart fuel which in the previous century had come to the rescue of a country threatened by the exhaustion of its wood supplies. Coal mining was transformed in no such revolutionary way as the textile and metal trades, but the use of steam pumping and hauling engines, wood props and safety lamps increased its capacities. No great expansion, however, was possible until transportation was reorganized. The great days of the English coalfields came with the construction first of canals, and then of railways and steamships. The annual output of coal was more than trebled between 1800 and 1845; twenty-five years later it was over 110 million tons, and the amount of coal exported was increasing in relation both to total exports and to the total output of coal.

The second phase of the industrial revolution, in which it became also a commercial revolution, began with the building of railways. The previous changes in transportation had every right to mark epochs, but they were too quickly superseded. Most of the great network of canals was dug in the half-century before 1815, but the era of hard turnpike roads, suitable for record runs by stage coaches, had hardly reached its prime when the railway age displaced it. Several important railway lines were built in the thirties; by 1840 the experiment was seen to have made good, and in the next few years thousands of miles were laid down. Steam transport by water had come earlier, but the United Kingdom had little more than 100 steamships in 1824, and less than 1,000 twenty years later, by which time ships were crossing the Atlantic under steam alone. The means of intercourse were further improved by the introduction of the penny post in 1840 and of the " electric telegraph " some seven years later.

The shipping of the United Kingdom showed practically no increase between the end of the war and 1840, but its tonnage rose from $2\frac{1}{2}$ millions in that year to over $4\frac{1}{2}$ millions in 1860. In considering the growth of British trade, allowance must be made for the fact that prices were falling at the rate of 10 per cent. per decade between 1820 and 1850, and after that rising. But it is noteworthy that the total exports of British products were practically of the same value in 1834 as in 1816; it took time for the war-racked Continent to recover sufficiently to buy British goods. After 1834 their value rose rapidly from 42 millions in that year to 71 millions in 1850 and 199 millions in 1870. The value of the foreign and colonial goods re-exported from Britain after importation was 18 millions in 1854, 44 millions in 1870. The total value of imports was 152 millions in 1854, 303 millions in 1870; the excess of these figures over the sum total of exports shows the colossal sums Englishmen were receiving in payment for their services as carriers by sea and as interest on capital invested abroad.

Well before the end of the eighteenth century London had supplanted Amsterdam as the financial capital of Europe, but as yet the field for investment was narrow. During the war the government's need of money gave golden chances to owners of capital, and after it every foreign country hoped to raise loans in the London market. Great financial houses like those of Rothschild and Baring became international forces. Capital was wanted at home too for commerce and industry, and was sought from the banks ; in certain cases joint-stock companies were formed, but it was not for some time, till the railway speculation of the forties in fact, that they became a common method of conducting business. Incorporation was made easier by an Act of 1844, but the principle of the limited liability of shareholders had to wait for recognition till the legislation of 1855–1862. Even so, private businesses remained the rule for another twenty or thirty years. Joint-stock banks were prohibited south of the Tweed, as infringing the Bank of England's monopoly, till 1826 ; an Act of that year, suggested by the failure of a number of private banks, allowed them outside a sixty-five mile radius from London; the distance limit was repealed in 1833 except as regards the issue of notes.

At the close of the war, not the Corn law itself was a more contentious issue than the currency. As in other spheres, men were being called upon to face problems of a nature and magnitude of which they had no experience. The government had been compelled to borrow largely to pay for the war, and there had been wild inflation. Since 1797 the Bank of England had not been bound to pay gold for notes, and notes had been issued in very large quantities. The Bullion Committee of 1810 had recommended that paper money should again be made convertible into gold, and this policy was finally carried out in 1821. It was fiercely criticized by those who, like William Cobbett, were indignant that capitalists who had lent to the government in the days of inflation should be repaid the full nominal value of their holdings now when money was dearer, and by others who, like Thomas Attwood, desired abundant money for industry. In the next twenty-five to thirty years, when trade was rapidly expanding, there was a shortage of currency due to the absence of any increase in the world's output of gold, and the period was one of falling prices. But at the time it was the danger of expansions of currency caused by irresponsible or ignorant bankers which seemed crucial. Before 1826 private banks had unrestricted power to issue notes; in that year the issuing of notes for less than five pounds was forbidden by law in England, but it was not till the Bank Charter Act of 1844 that the issue of notes even by the Bank of England was closely controlled. This Act, which incidentally stimulated the growing custom of payment by cheque, failed to avert the crisis of 1847; the Bank on this occasion adopted the expedient of raising its discount rate to 8 per cent.—a remedy not permissible before the recent repeal of the ancient usury laws. After 1850 the administration of the Bank improved notably in efficiency, and facilities for obtaining credit from banks and financial houses increased.

Such fragmentary facts and figures must serve as examples of the huge increase of wealth in England resulting from the transformation of agriculture, industry, transport, and commerce. This wealth was private wealth, as the energy which amassed it was individual energy. " The Industrial Revolution," says Professor Meredith, " was the work of a mere handful of men. Some ten or twelve individuals revolutionized, or created, each of a number of great industries." The use of capital was in those early days an adventurous act of faith : as individual enterprise enlarged the field of experiment and potential progress, so the absence of co-ordination and the reckless competition which it involved aggravated the risk of overproduction and glutted markets. In 1825, 1837, and 1847 there were commercial crises, followed as a rule by ruinous trade depression. Many ventures failed, but others brought in enormous returns and with them an exhilarating sense of mastery and achievement. Often the successful captain of industry had risen from the lowest rank. It was the romantic period in various spheres of life; certainly in business in England. Any freak of fortune seemed possible, and the prevailing spirit of optimistic self-reliance augured that wonders would not cease to occur nor prosperity to increase. The confidence in individual enterprise thus engendered was encouraged by the economic doctrine fashionable since Adam Smith. In Tudor and Stuart times the State had taken on itself to direct and regulate industry in the interests of the nation as a whole. Now *laissez-faire* was enthroned. In 1817 David Ricardo brought out his *Principles of Political Economy and Taxation*; his views had great influence both as expressed by himself and in the exaggerated form in which his pupils rendered them. Many, moreover, who did not share the Utilitarian rationalism of Benthamite theory agreed that regulation by the State had in practice often shown itself ignorant and harmful and might in many cases wisely be relaxed. But we cannot ignore the State, and it is time to consider what part it had played in the miracle.

In some cases positive action by parliament was needed to make individual initiative possible. Commons could not have been enclosed nor the commoners' rights taken away without

Enclosure Acts. Turnpike and Railway Acts gave facilities for the former and latter stages of the revolution in transport. Countless private Acts aimed at the reform of local administration by conferring special powers in special cases. Such legislation was required merely to start private enterprise on its course. More characteristic of this period are measures removing restrictions previously imposed by the State. Sometimes it was a matter of terminating a monopoly. The East India Company lost the sole right of trading with India in 1813, of trading with China in 1833; the curtailment of the monopoly of the Bank of England has been already mentioned, along with the repeal of the laws forbidding high rates of interest and hampering the growth of joint-stock enterprise. The development of fiscal policy was even more important.

At the end of the war the public expenditure of the United Kingdom had risen to over 110 millions a year, and the National Debt to 900 millions. The service of the debt exhausted about half the total revenue, and there was a deficit of over 30 millions. Taxes were cruelly heavy; about 40 out of the total of 67½ millions came from indirect taxation, but since 1803 a Property and Income Tax of two shillings in the pound had been levied. The insistence of the House of Commons on the prompt repeal of this detested tax, so " alien to the free spirit of the British constitution," set a hopeless task to successive Chancellors of the Exchequer who were anxious to reduce indirect taxation. Only on seven occasions in the next twenty-eight years was a deficit avoided. The Budgets, to use a recent phrase, of this period were based on a very complicated and quite unscientific prohibitive or protective tariff; duties which hampered trade more than they benefited the revenue were levied on several hundreds of articles, including raw materials, in accordance with the policy or caprice of a bygone age. In some instances, such as the duties on timber and sugar, there was an effective preference on colonial products. The Navigation Acts, relics of the Dutch wars of the seventeenth century, forbade trade with the colonies to any but British ships, and the importation of foreign goods into England to any but British ships or ships of the country of origin. Such a policy was bound to lead to retaliation by foreign Powers in favour of their own manufactures and shipping, and in several cases retaliatory measures had been threatened, if they had not been actually put into force.

This jungle of restrictive laws was cleared between 1820 and 1860, the greater part of it before 1850. The movement began with the London Merchants' petition of 1820, which in the authentic language of Free Trade declared "that the maxim of buying in the cheapest market and selling in the dearest, which regulates every merchant in his individual dealings, is strictly applicable as the best rule for the trade of the whole nation." A committee on foreign trade appointed by the House of Commons reported sympathetically, and within a few years drastic reforms were introduced. The excessive preference enjoyed by Canadian timber was cut down; prohibitive duties were repealed; duties on raw materials were reduced substantially, and duties on manufactured articles to a lesser degree. Free Trade was established between Ireland and Great Britain, their two Exchequers having been amalgamated in 1817. The Navigation Acts were simplified and relaxed to allow the colonies to trade direct with all countries—the United States already occupied a special position—and to enable concessions to be made to foreign shipping on a basis of reciprocity. Huskisson, the President of the Board of Trade, under whose auspices the chief of these reforms were enacted, was not a Free Trader; but he was in touch, as previous ministers had not been, with the mind of the business world which was now veering in a

Free Trade direction. The lowered tariffs did not diminish, but increased, the revenue, and when Peel found himself faced with a heavy deficit in 1841 after a long spell of trade depression, he followed in Huskisson's steps and went much further. His great Budget of 1842 again scaled down the tariff, involving changes in the rates on some 750 articles. To cover the temporary loss that would result from these reductions, Peel took the step no Chancellor of the Exchequer had dared to take for over twenty years: as a temporary measure, he imposed an income tax of sevenpence in the pound in Great Britain. The tax thus revived has never since been abolished; extended to Ireland in 1853, it became the chief item in the revenue. By 1844 consols, which had stood at 89 three years before, had risen to 99, and in 1845–6 Peel further revised the tariff, lowering the duties on manufactured articles to a general level of 10 per cent., and repealing altogether those on 430 articles, consisting largely of raw materials or supplying the food-stuffs, clothing, and comforts of the people. When in 1853 Peel's pupil, Gladstone, took the next important step in the same direction, he was able to show that Peel's policy of remitting indirect taxation had greatly increased the revenue, as it had reduced the cost of living.

Meanwhile the Navigation laws had been repealed, and the Corn laws, the citadel of Protection, had fallen to the onset of the armies of Manchester. How could import duties on corn be defended when duties on manufactured articles were being swept away ? Only on the ground that the landed interest was of such peculiar national importance as to deserve special privileges, even at the cost of keeping up the price of food in face of a growing population. This claim the middle classes would not admit, and by the end of 1845 the combined influence of Cobden's statistics and the spectre of Irish famine had converted Peel. Parliament, in repealing the Corn laws, recognized the fact that Britain was now primarily an industrial, not an agricultural, country.

The winning of Free Trade, the collapse of Chartism, England's immunity from contagion in the year of revolutions, and the vast possibilities of the railway and the telegraph,—all were infinitely gratifying to the class now acquiring the political hegemony, and all seemed to promise that the next half-century would be an era of peace and plenty. Richard Cobden was the prophet of their faith, and the Great Exhibition of 1851 its shrine and symbol. This millennial prospect was rudely shattered by the outbreak of the Crimean war. Shattered too was the seven years' programme of fiscal reform expounded to the House of Commons in 1853 in five hours of Gladstonian oratory. Nevertheless, for twenty years and more the expansion of British trade was regular and continuous, and wealth—except in unhappy Ireland—greatly increased, even if allowance be made for the rise in prices consequent on the influx of gold from North American and Australian mines. Railway construction had provided outlets for capital and labour, and even agriculture flourished. Untroubled as yet by foreign competition, Britain was reaping the fruits of industrial leadership.

The triumph of Free Trade reached its zenith in 1860, when Gladstone carried out a further reduction of the tariff, retaining duties, for revenue only, on less than fifty articles out of the thousand and more which had faced Peel eighteen years before ; at the same time Cobden crowned his prestige by negotiating with the French Emperor a commercial treaty which relaxed a needless fear of war between the two countries. For a time it seemed as if Peel and Cobden might be justified in their hopes that foreign governments would adopt free trade also ; there was a movement in Europe towards low tariffs, but nothing more. The vision remained unfulfilled. Finally in 1865 Gladstone had the satisfaction of reducing the tea-duty—over 2s. in 1840—to sixpence, and the income-tax, as an earnest of its eventual abolition, to fourpence; the national expenditure had risen to 66 millions from the fifty millions or so normal in the thirties and forties, but it was the lowest of any year since the Crimean war. The chief obstacle to the Chancellor's rigid economy, apart from actual war expenditure, had been the demand for an increase in armaments. Expenditure on national defence had fallen from over 71 millions in 1814 to less than 14 millions in 1822; in 1853, despite the cost of reviving the Militia and adapting the navy for steam, it was about sixteen millions. After the war it had risen, and by 1862, exclusive of war expenditure in China and the colonies and Palmerston's fortification policy, reorganization in both services, of which the building of ironclads was the chief feature, had raised it to $26\frac{1}{2}$ millions; of this sum over 15 millions were for the army, and over $11\frac{1}{4}$ for the navy.

Gladstone believed, and public opinion agreed with him, that the prosperity of all classes could best be secured by the reduction of taxation, direct as well as indirect, to the lowest possible point. He was not in favour of heroic measures of debt reduction nor of investing largely in social improvement. He trusted that prospering trade would provide steady employment and high wages, that increasing wealth would spread itself widely, and that a few taxes on articles of general consumption would suffice to meet necessary national expenses and gradually bring down the debt.

CHAPTER III

THE CONDITION OF ENGLAND QUESTION

How did the great outburst of energy suggested in the last chapter affect the welfare of the people? Did ordinary men and women share fairly in the increase of national prosperity? To ask such questions may seem absurd if one remembers the ghastly contemporary Reports on conditions of life and labour or the prophecies of revolution made by men like Francis Place in 1819 and Friedrich Engels twenty-five years later. Do not the rising of the southern farm labourers and the long menace of Chartism give all the answer needed? Before passing judgment there are several points to bear in mind. First, conditions differed widely between different industries and different localities; some were affected much sooner, or much more acutely, than others. Even if we can strike an average and discover a general tendency, individual cases will not lose their importance. There is no average man, and one man's happiness does not cancel another's misery, nor vice

versa. Secondly, we should distinguish so far
as we can between the period of transformation
and the time when the new dispensation had
established itself. Epochs of transition are usually
difficult and apt to cause suffering to those
without reserves to fall back upon. The period
we are considering made unique demands on the
people's power of adapting themselves to change.
The strain was accentuated by twenty years of
war, which hugely increased the cost of living
and made the first call on the Government's
attention ; and, apart from this, the whole
tendency of the thought of the day was un-
favourable to interference by the State in the
economic life of the nation. Thirdly, we must
keep our historical heads when we read of the
horrors described in the great Reports of the
Royal Commissions of the thirties and forties.
These descriptions may well arouse indignation,
but before apportioning it between individuals
we should compare the conditions not only with
our own standards but with those of an earlier
day. We may then possibly decide that what
was distinctive of the early nineteenth century
was not so much that men lived wretchedly as
that other men inquired into their wretchedness
and worked to relieve it. The eighteenth century did not wash its dirty linen in public records.
Lastly, we should remember that, while it is

difficult to measure welfare, it is impossible to measure happiness. One can only note the presence or lack of opportunities.

One or two facts which must have profoundly influenced social life are obvious : there were many more people in the island and a much greater proportion lived in towns. Adam Smith believed that " the most decisive mark of the prosperity of any country is the increase of the number of its inhabitants." Malthus in 1798 put forward views which were interpreted to mean that no permanent rise in the working man's standard of living was possible. Without accepting the former view, we may note, as against that of Malthus, that, though the population of Great Britain nearly doubled between 1811 and 1861, money wages increased while prices fell by nearly half. We may note also that from the beginning of the century onwards the principal cause of the increase in the population was not a rise in the birth-rate—the birth-rate was stationary or actually falling—but a fall in the death-rate which, though it rose slightly between 1810 and 1840, remained far below the level of the eighteenth century. In other words, people were living longer.

In Ireland, on a potato diet, the population was increasing, until the forties, twice as fast as in Great Britain, in spite of the outflow of

Irish labourers seeking work in England and Scotland. The potato famine of 1846–7 impelled a huge wave of emigrants to America, and thenceforward the population of Ireland continued to dwindle. In the Scottish Highlands and Islands, where the population had increased too fast even for its own wretched standard of living, a similar exodus from the crofts began about 1830 and continued till the end of the century.

As late as 1830 about half the population of Great Britain drew its livelihood from rural occupations, between a quarter and a third of the families in the island being returned as engaged in agriculture. About five-sevenths of these were labourers' families, and of the remainder rather less than half were those of occupiers who hired no labour. By the sixties less than a fifth of the male population was engaged in agriculture, and the number was shrinking absolutely as well as relatively.

The Land had been affected by two revolutions ; directly by the changes in farming and indirectly by those in industry, which squeezed out the old village industries and attracted labour to the towns by better wages. During the war landlords and farmers had flourished while labourers suffered cruelly. After the war all three classes suffered together. Men were dis-

missed and wages reduced, and owing to en-
closures and the factory system the man who in
earlier days might have struggled through by
eking out his income on by-employments now
found himself dependent on his wages alone.   In
many parts of the country nothing but the Poor
Law kept him from starving, and its operation,
demoralizing in the extreme to all, actually reduced many small occupiers to pauperism.   Dr.
Clapham estimates that over the country as a
whole the level of comfort was slightly higher
for the labourer of the mid-twenties than it had
been at the beginning of the war ; but in important areas it was lower, and beyond all question
the standard was miserable enough.   House-
room was scanty and bad ; dry bread and cheese
were the labourer's usual fare in the south—
potatoes were coming in in the twenties—and
there was a dearth of fuel.   The Game laws
helped the Corn laws to keep food scarce, and
it only needed the introduction of threshing-
machines and a couple of bad harvests to drive
the farm hands over a considerable part of the
south and east of England to open insurrection.
Night after night, in the winter months of 1830,
" Captain Swing " lit the sky with blazing ricks ;
half-starved labourers earning seven to nine
shillings a week smashed machines and demanded
money and a rise of wages with threats of vio-

lence. After the Yeomanry had easily suppressed this outbreak of despair, after the wages raised under duress had been reduced, there followed the vengeance of the law. Though no single life had been taken nor anyone even been seriously wounded, yet to atone for the damage to property and public order nine labourers were hanged and 457 transported to Australia, whence very few of them ever returned. The Whig government approved the sentences.

These memories were still fresh when the New Poor Law of 1834 put an end to the subsidizing of wages out of the rates. The Commissioners were unable to abolish out-relief entirely, but they greatly reduced it, and they were eminently successful in their design of making the pauper's lot so unpleasant that " independence " even with severe hardship should be regarded as preferable. The cost of poor-relief was cut down from nearly seven millions in 1830 to four-and-a-half millions in 1840, from 9s. 9d. to 6s. per head of the population ; but the labourer's last years were still pretty generally spent in the workhouse, the loathed " bastille " where he was parted from his wife and where the charity of the State was the coldest thing he had ever known. Will Cobbett, the countryman's philosopher and friend, the champion of the old England against the new, of farms against factories, of pigs against potatoes, lived just long enough to denounce this last intruding tyranny of Benthamism. Younger men were being driven to emigrate, and every year some tens of thousands crossed the ocean from ports in Great Britain. Improvement in the labourer's standard of living did come at length, but not till the early fifties after the crisis of the famine, when the reform of the tariff and the demand for railway labour had cheapened food and provided alternative employment. Naturally the existence of better paid trades near by reacted on agriculture, and it is not surprising to find wages in the industrial north markedly higher than in the southern counties.

The testimony of statistics, incomplete and often misleading as it must be, points to the same general conclusion in the case of the industrial worker. Generally speaking, industrial wages fell in and after the last years of the war and then remained fairly stationary from about 1830 till the middle of the century, after which they rose steadily till the sixties and later. This applies alike to the great unrevolutionized building trade, which employed more male labour than any other industry except agriculture, and to the cotton trade, though in the case of cotton, owing perhaps to the introduction of the self-acting mule, the fall continued during the later thirties. In the sixties the wages bill of the nation increased considerably more than twice as fast as the population. The cost of living for the working class, on the other hand, was falling fast from the end of the war till the early twenties, after which it remained pretty steady, with temporary rises about 1825, in the late thirties and in 1846-7. After 1847-8 it fell sharply, to start in 1853 on a gradual rise by no means equal to the rise in wages. The general result is that for the first thirty years of the peace the disorganization due to a period of change was not offset by any appreciable rise in the real wages of labour, for though prices were falling the commodities chiefly affected were not those consumed by the working classes. After 1850 commodities of the latter kind rose less than others, and the purchasing power of the wage-earners increased rapidly, as is attested by a greater volume of Savings Bank deposits and a higher consumption per head of tea and sugar.

Thus from the late forties onwards the poor were recovering from the economic effects of the war and the first shock of the industrial revolution. To this comforting generalization there are important exceptions, of which the most dramatic concerns the hand-loom weavers, in the cotton trade in particular. Here was an occupation, on which hundreds of thousands of workers were employed in the twenties, being slowly strangled after 1830 by the competition of the power-loom, while the surplus of labour was maintained by Irish workers with their low standard of life and skill. By mid-century the number of hand-loom weavers had shrunk to less than 50,000, and it is difficult to see how they lived on their miserable earnings. Even as it was, with no minimum wage, such as the weavers often demanded, enforced by law, unemployment was chronic and the only future for themselves or their children lay in change of occupation. This fact they were long reluctant to admit, but the trade depression which set in after 1836 killed hope, and by the forties they were yielding. Weavers in the other textile trades were affected similarly, but not so quickly. Among other industries suffering in the forties, though not from the use of machinery, were two alike in little else, framework knitting and coal mining.

So much for the wage-earner's means of livelihood; what of his surroundings? The first generation of workers in the newly concentrated industries were countrymen by origin, and even for their successors the family tradition was long rural. Country memories and habits and yearnings must have played their part in the discontent bred by the new urban conditions. By the middle of the century more than half the popu-

lation lived in towns, more than a third in seventy
towns of over 20,000 inhabitants.   It was in the
decade 1821–31 that the towns were growing at
the fastest rate, and at the end of the period the
outbreak of cholera called attention to their
horrible condition.   Thereafter a series of outspoken Reports forced the question of sanitation
to the front and produced the Public Health Act
of 1848 ; little was done however till after the
Crimean War.   It would seem that until about
1815 health conditions in the towns, as in the
country at large, were improving : cleanliness
increased—thanks partly to the new washable
cotton clothing—and some diseases were checked.
Then came the great influx into the towns ; no
proper measures were taken to deal with the
congestion, and the result was the horrors of
which we read in Chadwick's Reports and Engels'
indictment and which instilled much of its bitterness into the philosophy of Engels' friend, Karl
Marx.   We read of streets unpaved, undrained,
and uncleaned, of airless courtyards stinking
with refuse, of rivers serving as sewers, of families
crammed into jerry-built back-to-back houses
or damp cellars without ventilation or sanitation.
Water supply was not laid on till the fifties, and
soap and windows were taxed.   No wonder that
in five of the largest cities the death-rate rose
sharply in the thirties.   It was the nation's

tragedy that in these years of momentous change, when it was of supreme importance to posterity that the new setting of men's lives should be planned efficiently and with an eye to beauty, governments should be in power with neither the will nor the knowledge to control the mighty forces of capitalistic profit-making. The local authorities, such as they were, could not or would not cope with the apathy or corruption of the old interests or the thoughtless impetuosity of the new. The workers and voters of the future were doomed to grow up in ugliness, filth and crowded discomfort unassuaged as heretofore by the sight of trees and fields and the freshness of country air.

To the squalor and discomfort of slum life the factories added monotony, rigid discipline, and new fears of accident and disease, but they did not necessarily lower the standard of living. Conditions in the early textile mills were often scandalous, but so were conditions in the domestic handicrafts they supplanted, and the exploitation of child labour was nothing new. It should be remembered also that not for several decades after 1815 did the factories include more than a small minority of the wage-earning population, and that by the time factory work became common factory regulation had become usual too. It was the novelty of " these dark Satanic mills," and the comparative ease of supervising them, which most fortunately for the nation exposed them to denunciation and reform.

The new methods of industrial regulation began to be adopted just as Parliament cut away the last remnants of the great Elizabethan labour code. In the last years of the war the repeal of the laws ordering the fixing of wages by the Justices and the enforcement of apprenticeship left labour naked to the blast of competitive capitalism. In the first years of the peace the wind was tempered to the weakest by the first true Factory Act, due to the initiative of two enlightened employers, Sir Robert Peel, the elder, and Robert Owen. This Act established the principle of State interference with the employer; it was strengthened and extended by a series of statutes covering the whole half-century with which we are concerned. The Act of 1819 prohibited the labour of children under nine in cotton mills, but in them only. Children from five to six years old were at this time greatly in request as " piecers " in the steam mills established in populous districts, and they frequently worked fifteen or sixteen hours a day. Owing to inadequate provision for its enforcement, the Act had little effect; hence the importance of the Act passed by the first reformed parliament in 1833. Under the dual influence of rationalism and religion opinion was now becoming more humane. Sir Samuel Romilly and the younger Peel had begun to mitigate the barbarous follies of the criminal code, and even animals were receiving protection from the law. At length in 1830 the conscience of Yorkshiremen who had long worked for the abolition of negro slavery in the colonies was troubled by the thought of the child slaves in the mills at home. A powerful agitation was led by Robert Oastler and Michael Sadler in the north and supported in the House of Commons by Lord Ashley, later Earl of Shaftesbury, who became from henceforward the industrial workers' parliamentary champion. The Act of 1833 applied to textile mills generally ; it extended protection to " young persons " under eighteen, and it set up four government inspectors empowered to enter factories and make rules and instructed to report regularly to the Home Office. This all-important provision, suggested by certain mill-owners and scorned by the operatives, has in fact proved the key to the success of the British system of factory legislation, which the world has copied. It not only made it possible to enforce the law, but it provided a source of accurate and impartial information.

The Factory Acts of 1819 and 1833 were isolated measures ; those of 1844 and 1847 were part of a great corpus of social legislation, based on official inquiry, by which government was now coming to grapple, however incoherently, with the " condition of England " question. Ashley's Mines Act of 1842, passed with unusual promptitude within a few months of the appearance of a horrifying Report, applied the methods of the modern conscience to an old unrevolutionized industry. Colliery owners were no longer to allow children of seven and under, or women, to work like animals underground. In protecting the interests of grown-up women this measure broke new ground. Two years later another Factory Act, providing for the compulsory fencing of dangerous machinery, extended to women in the mills the protection hitherto enjoyed by " young persons." In 1847 the Ten Hours Act, applying in the letter to these two classes only, but in practice, eventually, to men also, was hailed as the crown of thirty years' agitation.

The fact that, sixty years after parliament first intervened to protect pauper apprentices in factories, children might still be forced to work at the age of five or six for long hours in warehouses and private workrooms, and scarcely older in potteries or on making matches and explosives, shows the weakness of the British bit-by-bit methods. It was much easier, however, to regulate labour in factories than labour at home, and even in the lace and hosiery trades, which by the sixties were largely dependent on power-machines, certain processes were carried on at home or in private houses. In fact, said the Commissioners of 1862, " against no persons do the children of both sexes so much need protection as against their parents." But it was not only children that needed protection. Some 750,000 women and girls were employed in the dressmaking trades, often in overcrowded work-rooms and sometimes for sixteen hours a day. Eventually in 1864 and 1867 government measures extended the Factory Acts to numerous industries not carried on in factories, such as blast furnaces, foundries and forges—to all in fact where fifty or more persons worked together on any manufacturing process—while corresponding regulations were made for smaller establishments, including a prohibition of work in any handicraft by children under eight. How hard it might be to enforce the law when made, is shown by the failure of a succession of measures passed during our period to prevent the occasional burning or suffocation of sweeps' climbing boys in the difficult chimneys of large houses. Householders were loath to admit, and legislators to enjoin, interference with the privacies of an Englishman's home even to save the lives of the defenceless.

The results thus achieved were won against the persistent opposition of would-be economists, of manufacturers and, in the first stages, of Ministers. Resistance was fiercest in the thirties and forties, after the Reform Act had encouraged the rich middle class and before the new regulation had justified itself in practice. Opponents relied not so much on the abstract error of interfering with the worker's freedom—though no doubt the reluctance to regulate *adult* labour was due to this feeling—as on the handicap which restriction would place on British industry while its rivals abroad were unrestricted. In the debates of the sixties such arguments of principle hardly figured. Theories had yielded to experience in a world becoming more and more reconciled to the idea that the State might act for good as well as for evil.

Theory had proved wrong in another matter of equal importance. Alongside the increasing efficacy of factory legislation must be set the development of self-help through organization for collective bargaining. Here the workers asked of the State only that it should repeal the restrictions it had imposed. Since 1799 it had been a criminal offence, punishable by imprisonment, for workmen to " combine " for the purpose of keeping up wages or reducing hours of work. The Act applied on paper to combinations of masters also, but was in practice never enforced against them; nor was it enforced against the men strictly enough to prevent the continued existence of many trade clubs and unions, especially among the more aristocratic handicrafts. But many prosecutions for "conspiracy" took place; the law drove trade unionism underground and greatly weakened the bargaining power of labour at a time when it needed every ounce of strength. Thanks to the energy and organizing ability of Francis Place, more than any other man, and to the growing distrust of laws restricting free trade, these iniquitous provisions were repealed in 1824–5, and the right of collective bargaining was expressly recognized. The prohibition on skilled artisans to seek their fortunes abroad was repealed at the same time.

The new freedom mounted to the heads of labour. A series of disastrous local strikes was followed in 1829 by a sudden immense expansion of trade union ambitions. John Doherty, the cotton spinner, began to organize on a national scale, not in his own industry only, and conceived the idea of including all the wage-earners in the country in one huge union. The National Association for the Protection of Labour, founded in 1830, led on to the Grand National Consolidated Trades Union, with its half million members, aiming at a dramatic improvement of the lot of all workers by the achievement, through the instrumentality of a general strike, of a universal eight-hour day, if not of a new order of society established on co-operative lines.   The exciting events of the struggle for political reform, and disappointment with the Whig Reform Act, lured the simple working men of the time into the new venture.   Its prophet was Robert Owen, the self-made cotton employer from New Lanark, whose striking success in his own model village and mills had convinced him that society could be transformed in a single generation by the power of education, could only the spirit of competition yield to that of co-operation.   Owenism, the first form of modern British socialism, had spread deeply, if not very widely, among the wage-earners in the previous decade, and most of the working-class leaders had been inspired by his boundless faith.   To the upper and middle classes trade unionism seemed not only to violate economic law but to be something uncanny and terrible, and its sudden expansion in these years caused intense fear.   Only terror born of ignorance can explain the sentence of transportation for seven years—actually served for four years—passed on six Dorchester labourers for the mere act of administering an oath of admission.   Such dangers and the active counter-attack of many employers, taken with their own vagueness of aim and inexperience, sufficed to bring the hopes of the new unionists crashing to the ground before the end of 1834. It was the end not of an episode only but of an epoch. Numbers rapidly shrank, and with them the scale of the trade unions' activities and purpose. Local trade clubs, totalling hardly 100,000 members in the whole country, eschewed political and social ambitions and devoted themselves, with little success in the slump of the later thirties, to the safeguarding of their standard of living. Trade unions took little part, as such, in the Chartist movement, and when the general proletarian excitement died down in the early forties we find them disclaiming aggressive aims, even deprecating strikes and advocating " a good understanding between the employer and the employed." On this pacific basis a generation of skilful officials, following the example of the Engineers, built up national craft organizations of unprecedented wealth and strength, despite the repeated efforts of employers to force work-men out of their unions. In the sixties the London " Junta " of five able working men, with the help of the new Trades Councils, con-trived to make the weight of trade unionism felt effectively in parliamentary politics. The amend-ment, in 1867, of the law of Master and Servant, under which a workman had been punishable by imprisonment for breaking a contract of service, is described as " the first positive success of trade unionism in the legislative field." But by this time lock-outs and strikes, the latter sometimes accompanied by violence, had brought the whole question of the position of trade societies into debate, and in 1867 the subject was referred to a Royal Commission.

In the days when combination for industrial purposes was still illegal, trade unions had sometimes masqueraded as Benefit Societies, and the insurance side of their work remained an important one. Friendly Societies, formed for this purpose only, had already a membership of 900,000 in 1815, and thirty years later, after the Oddfellows and other great Orders had been founded, were approaching the figure of a million and a half. Meanwhile the Rochdale pioneers had founded the Co-operative movement, the only permanent offspring of Owen's great idea. Various producers' associations, such as he had pictured, had been born and died, but this venture of 1844, with its principal object of supplying cheap groceries to its members, was on different lines. The system spread rapidly in the manufacturing districts of northern England and the Scottish midlands, and twenty years later the Co-operative Wholesale Society was founded, to some degree realizing the wider hopes of the early pioneers.

Thus by the sixties the more enterprising at least of the wage-earners had been prepared for full citizenship by long practice in managing important concerns of their own—the best possible form of political education. Of education in the narrower sense they had had little, for the provision made for it in England in the early nineteenth century was typical of the social life of the time. In Scotland a national system of parish schools put the elements of education—and Latin—within the reach of the poorest, and access to one of the four hard-living, hard-thinking universities was easy. England lagged far behind. The great inventors were not the product of a country organized for intellectual adventure. An attempt to introduce something like the Scottish system of elementary education had been rejected by the Lords in 1807, when it was made clear that the poor were not intended by their masters to think. For the sons of the ruling classes the Public Schools supplied a training in courage and character, in patriotism and oratory, but in few of the other requirements of statesmanship; at the two universities, reserved in the main for Churchmen, classics and mathematics could be studied further, and some men took advantage of the unique opportunities for intellectual intercourse offered by the college system. The children of the lower orders, apart from such instruction as they might obtain as apprentices or in Sunday School, had but scanty chances of education even after the foundation, in the last years of the war, of two rival societies, undenominational and Anglican respectively, for the purpose of supplementing the old charity schools and dames' schools. Thanks to the mutual suspicions of Churchmen and Dissenters, not a penny, until the Reform Act, was contributed by the State. The lack was especially scandalous in the new industrial areas, where as late as the forties no attempt had been made to meet the needs of the growing population. But education was in the air, with Robert Owen, Henry Brougham, and the Benthamites as its champions, and nearly all the social movements we have noticed cared greatly for it. University and King's Colleges were founded in London in the twenties; shortly before, the foundation of the first Mechanics' Institutes laid the base of adult education. In 1833 the State intervened in two ways: by making a small grant, which became annual, in subvention of voluntary schools, and by instructing the new inspectors to enforce the school attendance of factory children. By 1861 the percentage of illiteracy in England had fallen to 24·6 of the

male and 34·7 of the female population ; the
figures for Scotland were 10·6 and 21·3, and for
the Irish people as a whole 53. It can hardly
have been the delights of learning which com-
pensated the poor for the rigours of the hard
times.

Nor had they much opportunity for recreation,
whether of mind or body. Cheap editions were
as yet unknown, and even newspapers were hard
to come by. From 1819 to 1833, when the tax
was lowered, an ordinary newspaper cost sevenpence, and there was a duty on paper till 1861.
The decay of rural life put an end to such enter-
tainments as Thomas Hardy pictures in his
Wessex cottages and on village greens, and
factory hours gave little leisure for the games
which the old part-time employments had
allowed. To countless families dancing and
plays were sin, and in the evening there was no
alternative to the public-house.

Aghast at the anarchy of her economic life
and the feebleness of her government, the eminent
French historian of England in the nineteenth
century finds the elements of cohesion and
stability in her religion alone ; not, to be sure,
in the official influence of the Established Church,
still in large measure apathetic and absentee,
nor yet in the weakening tradition of the old
Nonconformist congregations, but in the spirit

and power of the Methodist revival. Spreading
far beyond the circles of its professed adherents,
the gospel of Methodism brought solace and
hope to thousands, and taught poor men to
endure " as seeing him who is invisible." For
unlike the militant Puritanism of the seventeenth century, the aggrieved Dissent of the
eighteenth, or the eager intellectualism of the
Scottish Kirk, the new movement helped not
the radical but the conservative side in politics.
Not only did the elaborate organization of the
Methodists demand and inculcate discipline, but
ever since the French Revolution radicalism had
been tainted with irreligion. Methodists were
reminded to honour the King as well as to fear
God. And fortunately for the established order
the new piety was strongest in just those classes
and districts from which it had most to fear—
among the skilled artisans and lower middle
class and in the industrial areas of Wales and
northern England where the Church counted for
little. Thus it was the influence of Whitefield
and the Wesleys, so M. Halévy believes, which
neutralized the effect of the careers of Watt and
Arkwright, of Eldon and Sidmouth, of Malthus
and Ricardo, of Cobbett and Owen and Feargus
O'Connor.

But the effects of the Evangelical revival were
not merely negative. It did not only spread

belief in the sinfulness of man and fear of hell-fire. Aflame with the Christian love which it had rekindled, Churchmen like Wilberforce and Ashley, for all their dislike of democracy, worked incessantly for the salvation of the oppressed, combining with the free-thinking Benthamites whose inspiration came from those very French principles which the Churchmen detested. It was these two streams of thought, blent with the good sense of practical statesmen like Peel, which gradually washed away the foundations of the ancient citadel of folly and wrong and restored internal peace.

The generation after Waterloo was a cruel time for the poor, but from the early twenties things began slowly to improve, in Great Britain if not in Ireland. First came the legal, fiscal, and administrative reforms of Romilly, Huskisson, and Peel, with the emancipation of trade unions ; then the great crop of Whig-Radical measures which followed the Reform Act ; then in the forties the dramatic reforms of the Peel epoch—free imports, factory and mine laws, cheap food, and the first Public Health Act, while the vast construction of railways found employment for labour, increased mobility, and opened a new era of prosperity. We have now to see how the great political changes came about.

CHAPTER IV

THE MOVEMENT TOWARDS DEMOCRACY

ENGLAND, like most other countries, has had but short experience of democracy. In 1815 the word was a bogey to the great majority of the people : it suggested barricades, and bad money, and the guillotine, and was one of the perils which the British constitution stood to avert. Under that constitution England enjoyed in theory a " mixed form of government " —an ideal blend of the monarchical, the aristocratic, and the popular elements : but in fact she was ruled, as she had been ruled since the Revolution, by a hereditary aristocracy—an aristocracy still consisting mainly of landowners but much diluted latterly by merchants, bankers, and some captains of industry. Control of the County Bench and of both houses of parliament made it supreme in local and national affairs alike.

Until 1830 the government was in the hands of the Tory party, reinforced during the war and after by successive adhesions of Whigs. They were strong in the support of the Church, the Land, the princes of finance and commerce, and many industrial magnates. The party had a die-hard and a liberal wing : it was united in opposing any general reform of the representative system, but divided on the question—supremely important in Ireland—of admitting Roman Catholics to parliament. The feeble Opposition was agreed in advocating Catholic Relief, but was undecided on the Reform question and on much else. In its ranks was the Whig section of the aristocracy, faithful to the tradition of Charles Fox, but unable to furnish the people with either a programme or a leader ; their old allies, the Nonconformists of the towns ; certain circles of business and professional men who felt no devotion to Whig doctrine, and to whom the foreign name of " Liberals " was coming to be applied ; and the Radical Reformers, or Radicals, to be counted on the fingers of one hand in the House of Commons, all to a greater or less extent influenced by the ideas of Jeremy Bentham.

Though parties existed and had their traditions, they lacked organization and sharp definition. Until it divided on the Address, it was not known how a newly elected House would declare itself, and members were far less bound than now by party allegiance in their voting. In 1816 a Tory House of Commons insisted on repealing the Income Tax against the wishes of the Tory government. In 1827 Canning, the enlightened Tory, took office with the support of the more liberal, but the distrust of the more orthodox, wings of both great parties, and it is possible that, had the Reform Bill not clarified issues, a system of smallish parliamentary groups would have established itself.

Besides the sense of parliament, a government had to reckon with the Sovereign and with public opinion. In spite of Pitt's ascendancy and George III's long illness, the royal will was far from negligible ; at a crisis it might prove a serious obstruction. The King's assent was never refused to a bill which had passed both Houses, but no measure to which he objected could be introduced by his ministers, and his dislike could keep a man permanently out of office. Neither the prerogative of dissolution, nor that of creating peers, was exercised, as of course, on ministers' advice. Within the Cabinet solidarity was the accepted rule, though the Duke of Wellington enjoyed a detachment of his own ; but since the deaths of Pitt and Fox the prestige of the Premiership had declined, and the position of the Sovereign was accordingly strengthened.

The story of the various ways and increasing degree in which public opinion outside contrived

to force changes on the government and legislature, until at length it found more adequate
expression in parliament, is the main theme of
this chapter. In the eighteenth century its
pressure was violent in proportion to its un-
certainty and intermittence. The recognized
methods of constitutional influence were elections, county meetings, and petitions. Owing to
the imperfections of the representative system,
elections were in no true sense appeals to the
nation; yet in all but the closest of rotten
boroughs a strong wave of popular feeling had
some effect, and there were a few important
constituencies where the franchise was thor-
oughly democratic. County meetings could only
be held under the auspices of the aristocracy,
but they showed the drift of agricultural opinion,
and petitions to parliament might prove useful
advertisements. Outside these methods an occasional riot might warn the government to look
where it was going, but continuous organized
agitation for political ends was the invention of
the generation after Waterloo.

Among the men who created and first used
the new weapons Francis Place and William
Cobbett stand foremost. Place was a London
tailor, proud, honest, and efficient, with a hard
clear mind; a shrewd judge of character and of
the practical. A born wire-puller, he devoted

himself in 1807 to reorganizing the democratic Westminster electorate in the Radical interest. Experience gave him a unique knowledge of the political desires and capacities of the London working man, and convinced him that, however much he might despise the middle classes, nothing could be done without their co-operation. Himself a disciple of Bentham and of the " classical " school of economists, he had no faith in socialism or trade unionism ; but for nearly fifty years he was one of the mainsprings of the democratic movement.

Far more conspicuous in both person and career was Cobbett, the burly tribune of the country-side and as good a hater as English politics have known. His bonnet hummed with bees, but from the end of the war onwards he had the intuition to concentrate on reform of parliament, of the most radical brand, and to make his primary appeal to the working class. Like other demagogues of his time he toured the country as a stump orator, but it is as the father of cheap popular journalism that Cobbett is most memorable. In 1816 he reduced the price of his *Register* to twopence ; the so-called " Twopenny Trash " enjoyed a circulation immense for those days, and was remarkably successful in stimulating political interest among working men. In 1819 parliament imposed a fourpenny stamp on all newspapers costing less than sixpence, but by mingled ingenuity and effrontery Cobbett contrived to make his trumpet still heard.

The early years of the French Revolution had inspired the foundation of political clubs, based very likely on the elaborate Methodist organization, in different layers of English society. These had been suppressed by Pitt, and even when times became calmer it needed caution to join any such body without breaking the law. Nevertheless, " Hampden Clubs " were formed with impunity in different parts of the country, and these too played their part in the awakening of democratic opinion. Trade union influence on politics in this period was slight.

During the twenties the cause of constitutional reform made gradual though silent progress ; but it was events in Ireland which brought matters to a head and incidentally set a new precedent for political agitators. In 1824 Daniel O'Connell founded the " Catholic Association " in Ireland, and financed it by the " Catholic Rent." He had long worked for the repeal of the Union with Great Britain ; he now concentrated his efforts on the demand that Roman Catholics should be made eligible for parliament. " Emancipation," as it was called, had eloquent advocates even among Tory ministers, and half the House of Commons was favourable ; but it was not till O'Connell aroused the Irish peasantry to shake off their landlords' political control and threatened to make government in Ireland impossible, that the Tory leaders, Wellington and Peel, became convinced that the concession must be made.   It was made in 1829, and its result was to split the Tory party, already weakened by recent divisions and defections as well as by over twenty years of unchallenged power.

After the Irish bombshell came the French. While the elections required by the death of George IV in the summer of 1830 were actually taking place, news arrived that the party of reaction had been struck down in Paris, and the king driven from his throne after three days of revolutionary fighting.   More important still, no excesses had followed on the victory of the populace, and English Reformers rejoicing in the defeat of absolutism could point to a revolution achieved without massacre or madness.   The Opposition were mightily encouraged, and with good cause ;   soon after parliament met in November, a reckless declaration by the Duke of Wellington against any change whatever in the representative system sounded the knell of his ministry and rang in ten years of Whig government.   Lord Grey, the Duke's successor, was a Whig of the Whigs, an aristocrat distrustful of the people but convinced of the need for change. Despondent and inert in opposition, he proved himself a firm, patient, and statesmanlike Prime Minister. The ministry which he now formed for the express purpose of carrying a reform of parliament showed small trace of radicalism, yet it produced a bill which astonished friends and foes alike by its boldness.

The unreformed House of Commons was unrepresentative of the nation in three ways. In the first place the distribution of seats was arbitrary : the southern counties were enormously over-represented with regard to their population and wealth, and many unimportant villages returned two members each, while Birmingham, Leeds and Manchester had none. Secondly, the distribution of votes in the constituencies was arbitrary : in the counties only forty-shilling freeholders had the franchise ; in the boroughs there was no uniformity, but nearly everywhere the electors were but a tiny section. Thirdly, in many boroughs and some counties a few wealthy or otherwise powerful individuals could, by corruption or influence, secure the election of whom they would ; seats were openly spoken of as property and had their known price. In Scotland there were no popular constituencies at all. In Ireland the county electorates were large, but usually dependent on the landlords' wishes, while practically every borough was under the control of a patron. The main features of the Whig proposals were to disfranchise many small boroughs; to give members to the most important of the large towns and more members to some counties; to establish a uniform £10 rating qualification in all boroughs, and slightly to extend the suffrage in the counties. Though little calculated, in fact, to disturb aristocratic predominance, the Reform Bill struck a deadly blow at prescriptive rights; and though it only enfranchised portions of the middle class, increasing the electorate from 435,000 to 655,000, it established a precedent for enfranchising other classes in course of time. Despite absurd hopes and fears, it was rightly recognized by the country as a measure of profound importance, and the working men who supported it, though it brought them no immediate advantage, showed a sound instinct.

The struggle for " the Bill, the whole Bill, and nothing but the Bill " was long, fierce and dramatic. It was fought on the floor of both Houses, on the hustings, and in the King's closet. Every resource of the constitution, and popular methods as yet unknown to it, were employed before the bill became law. Opposition in the Commons was defeated by a surprise dissolution, by which appeal was made to the electorate in a manner almost without precedent. Opposition in the Lords was defeated by the threat of creating some eighty additional peers, the reluctant king not complying till the impossibility of forming an alternative government had been demonstrated. In the background throughout, but not far off, was the menace of forcible action on the part of the populace in the great towns, a populace displaying unexampled interest in politics and organized with unexampled efficiency. It was the first time, said Francis Place, that the people had ever " combined of their own free will for a really national purpose." They were convinced that they possessed " the moral power to control the government." How had they acquired it ?

The financial and commercial crash of 1825–6 had led to cuts in wages and loss of employment. In 1829 there were acute distress and discontent in many parts of the country. The first great expansion of trade union activity was beginning, and the theories of Robert Owen and the other early English socialist writers were fermenting in men's minds. Cobbett found audiences in the north very favourable to Reform. In London a Radical Reform Association was founded, with a " Radical Rent " of a penny, copied clearly from O'Connell. In the next few months societies to promote parliamentary reform broke out in many different places. Much the most important of these was the Birmingham Political Union, founded at a huge public meeting in January, 1830, on the initiative of Thomas Attwood, an inflationist banker of great local influence who rose in the course of the Reform struggle to the position of a national hero. The Birmingham Union and many of its imitators were based on the co-operation of enthusiasts from both middle and working classes, and though alarming to the official mind, they supported the Whig bill and remained respectably legal. Other Unions were confined to working men and denounced the bill as a sham, hardly disguising their desire for the overthrow of the existing constitution. But it was partly the wisdom and partly the good fortune of the Whigs to produce a measure at once just moderate enough to secure the approval of parliament and just drastic enough to conciliate the vast majority of the politically minded classes without. In organizing and disciplining these, in alternately arousing and restraining them, the Political Unions played an essential part ; it was largely due to the efforts of men like Attwood and Place that so much agitation was accompanied by so little violence, when violence would have gravely prejudiced the cause of Reform. There had been no such organization in English history, and here lies the true importance of this episode in the development of democracy.

To us the Reform Act is significant as marking the first breach in the wall of aristocracy ; to the Whigs its supreme virtue was its finality. They looked on the circumstances attending its passing as wholly exceptional and desired no fundamental change in the ways of government. Nevertheless, there were some things which had to be done, some changes demanded by the March of Mind, and for a few years the Whigs were the vehicles of alien forces. Local government was drastically reconstructed ; the weak factory law was strengthened ; slavery was abolished in the Empire ; public money was granted for education ; the duties on newspapers were reduced ; and the penny post was inaugurated. There were other things that had to be done, but the Whigs were not the men to do them. Financial policy needed overhauling, but the Whigs knew little of finance, and one deficit followed another in their budgets. When they turned to Ireland, in chronic disturbance and dominated by O'Connell, the established Church crouched like a lion in the path and rent them asunder. Finally, they lacked both the courage and the will to assert the legislative supremacy of the Commons against the reviving destructiveness of the Lords. But two great services they

F

rendered to the Empire before their unlamented fall in 1841. When faced by rebellion in Canada, they sent out the boldest of their number, Lord Durham, to cope with the situation, and through the tactful promptings of Lord Melbourne they instilled into the mind of the girl who became queen in 1837 those Whig maxims of constitutional monarchy and royal self-suppression which alone could harmonize with the rising political thought of the age.

The Tories had fought the Reform Bill tooth and nail, not because they thought the old system perfect, but as fearing that so sweeping a measure would change the character of the ancient constitution they reverenced and make all government impossible. The old system did at least work, whereas they had no confidence in either the Whigs or the £10 householders. The immediate future of the party rested in the hands of Sir Robert Peel. It is his glory to have accepted the new situation, to have cut loose from reactionary Toryism, and to have built up a Conservative party ready to reform " every institution that really required reform." Reduced to a hundred and fifty in 1832, when it seemed possible that the official Opposition to the Whigs might be the Radicals, Peel and his followers soon established themselves as the only possible alternative government ; when the

Whigs fell, they came triumphantly into power and for five years ruled the country with an efficiency and conscientiousness it had probably never known before.

The disappointment of the wild hopes bred by the Reform Bill in the minds of democrats turned their energies into various channels. After the collapse of the premature trade union-ism of 1829–34, the attention of public-spirited working men was divided between the campaign for a cheap press, the continued agitation for a ten-hour day in the factories, and impassioned protest against the new Poor Law. Then once again distress engendered by trade depression unloosed a mass assault on two fronts. The political and social aspirations of the industrial proletariat took shape in the demand for the People's Charter, while the northern manufac-turers attacked the Corn laws which the landed interest regarded as the palladium of its pre-dominance.

In 1836–7 the disillusioned enthusiasts of the extreme Left had returned to political agitation. The societies formed at the time of the Reform struggle were revived or copied, and a slogan was soon found in the six points of the Charter, a document drafted with the help of Place by William Lovett, an educated working man of the trade-union-secretary type. The six points

were Manhood Suffrage, Annual Parliaments,
Voting by Ballot, Equal Electoral Districts,
Payment of Members, and the abolition of a
property qualification for parliament ; they were
the traditional Radical demands of more than
forty years earlier.   If the London Radicals supplied Chartism with a programme, its organization was borrowed from Birmingham, where
Attwood and his Political Union were again on
the warpath ; but its thousands of devotees and
the faith and fire which sustained them came
from the industrial north.   Here the miseries of
the hand-loom weavers and frame-knitters, the
grievances of those whom the factories over-
worked and of those whom they deprived of
work, and the new brutality of the Poor Law,
had incited a real insurrectionary fervour.   The
proletarian reaction to the asperities of the
industrial revolution, foreshadowed in 1815-19
and encouraged by the events of 1830-2, was
now ripe for violent expression.   There were
monster meetings in the north, often by torch-
light ;   there were fiery speeches and printed
manifestoes ;   there were sittings of Conventions,
and mammoth petitions to parliament, and
threats of a general strike ; there were, in fact,
isolated outbreaks of armed insurrection, and
but for the vigilance, tact, and firmness of Sir
Charles Napier, the military commander, much

more serious risings would have occurred. But though on three separate occasions matters came to a head, and something terrific was expected to happen, the leaders always drew back and the movement ended in fiasco. Indeed, that very agitation of 1830-2, which the Chartist leaders regarded as their season of training and rehearsal, had by its success foredoomed their own movement to failure.

Then middle and working classes had been united. Now sufficient of the former had been enfranchised to make the Act of 1832 appear to the country at large an adequate instalment of reform. The middle class were now set against revolution, and indeed what the bulk of the working men desired was not revolution nor any specific political change, but an improvement in their conditions of life. Chartism flourished when distress increased, in 1838, 1842, 1847, but languished when it abated. Even those extremists who desired revolution by force had neither the leaders nor the organization nor the cohesion to carry it through. They were indeed unlucky in their chiefs, a rash, incompetent, cowardly crew, who by their silly mouthings disgusted moderate people and, not least, sincere democrats like Lovett and Place. Feargus O'Connor, the god of the later Chartism, was as wretched a hero as incense ever intoxicated. In

1838 he assured his dupes that "universal suffrage would at once change the whole character of society from a state of watchfulness, doubt and suspicion to that of brotherly love, reciprocal interest and universal confidence." "Six months after the Charter is passed," he said in 1842, "every man, woman and child in the country will be well fed, well housed, and well clothed." He died insane in 1855.

Chartism was not a purely working-class, nor even a purely Radical, movement. It was a matter of feeling rather than of thought, and attracted men of very different creeds : Place, the adherent of *laissez-faire* economics ; Oastler, the Tory opponent of child-labour and the Poor Law ; Lovett, the Owenite Co-operator, who, accepting the new industrial society as permanent, worked on this basis to raise the condition of his fellows ; O'Connor, the Irish visionary, who protested blindly against it and cherished vague ideas of resettling the people on the land. Its historical importance lies in its having been "the first genuinely democratic movement for social reform in modern history," which as such influenced Karl Marx and Continental socialists ; it further aroused the class-consciousness of the working men—the "fustian jackets, blistered hands and unshorn chins"— to whom O'Connor appealed, bequeathing them a legacy of hopes unfulfilled, of memories and of martyrs.

As Chartism was the spectacular failure, so the Anti-Corn Law League was the spectacular success, of political agitation in the forties. The aims of Chartism were vast and vague ; those of the League limited and definite. The League was strong, where Chartism was weak, in leadership and organization. While Chartism was primarily a working-class, the League was primarily a middle-class movement ; but whereas the differences between Chartists from the middle and working classes tended to increase, the League gradually extended its influence among working men. Its source and centre was Manchester, and in history it stands personified in one man, Richard Cobden, the self-made calico-printer, in many respects the epitome of the middle-class Victorian Liberal. Very serious, very public spirited, supremely confident in the destiny of his country, his class and himself, he believed that free trade between nations was the secret of peace, and that " a moral and even a religious spirit " might " be infused into the topic of the Corn Laws." This moral fervour for a fiscal principle was something new in politics ; combined in Cobden's case with complete mastery of detail and a gift of lucid argument, in that of his brother in arms, John Bright, the Quaker cotton-spinner, with oratorical genius and a majestic simplicity, it proved itself a mighty force on British platforms.   In September, 1841, the two friends vowed never to rest till the Corn law was repealed, and they kept their vow. The obstacles were immense : the concentrated opposition of the landowners entrenched in parliament ; the dislike and contempt felt by upper and lower classes alike for cotton lords and factory tyrants ; the jealousy of the Chartists against wealthier and more efficient agitators. But by dint of tireless speechmaking and an unceasing flow of able pamphlets the spokesmen of the League convinced first the middle classes, then the town working men, then the farm labourers and even a number of the farmers, and finally, with the elements conspiring to help them, the Tory Prime Minister himself, that the tax on imported wheat must be repealed if the rising population was not to starve.   Nothing had been seen in Europe before like this sustained intensive campaign of argument, backed by elaborate organization that left nothing to chance, and Cobden found himself the oracle and model of foreign democrats.   The feat of the League was indeed unique.   The Reformers of 1831 had succeeded, but they had had the government and a fair portion of the aristocracy on their side ; the Chartists, with no such help, had failed miserably; Cobden and Bright, improving on O'Connell's example, had won by persuasion alone against the massed forces of the governing class.

The repeal of the Corn laws was of signal importance in the development of the English parties no less than of English democracy. The League might convince Peel, but Peel could not convince his followers nor even all his colleagues. Stanley left him, to replace him as leader of the Conservative party, and Benjamin Disraeli won his spurs by inciting "the gentlemen of England" to drive from office the chief who had betrayed them. They had sat restive for some time under his enlightened rule, but without the young Jew's genius they would hardly have revolted; their action was a complete surprise to Peel himself. Peel's career was a strange one: twice, in 1829 and in 1845, he felt compelled by facts to pass, as a Minister, measures of cardinal importance which he had long opposed; in each case he—or those who refused to follow him—broke the party and let in the Opposition for long spells of power. It was not an experience to encourage a Conservative statesman to hope to lead the party from the left. Yet a man with longer sight might have fared better. Unrivalled in administrative skill and the adroit handling of immediate parliamentary difficulties,

Peel failed curiously in forecasting the future. He was only sixty-two when he died in 1850, having done more than any other man to raise the standard of English public life. The small but distinguished group who changed with him on the Corn laws retained the name of Peelites for some seven years longer, but, apart from providing a bridge for their most eminent member, Gladstone, to cross to the Liberal side, their existence only added to the weakness of governments. The Conservatives were left diminished in numbers and sadly deficient in men of ability. The Whigs, who took office under Lord John Russell in 1846, passed some valuable measures and weathered the squalls of the year of revolutions ; but the virtue, such as it was, had gone out of Whiggism, and the leaders were as yet afraid of being democrats. After a brief Conservative interlude and a spell of coalition government under the pacific Peelite Aberdeen, which let the country " drift " into the Crimean war, the strong man Palmerston took the helm, and retained it with one short interval until his death in 1865.

The eighteen years which followed the final collapse of Chartism were placid as they were prosperous. Whether Whigs or Tories were in power, and generally it was the Whigs, the government was conservative and its inertia reflected the general contentment. Free trade reconciled the bulk of the middle classes to their rulers, and improving conditions pacified the working men. But the epoch of strife just ended had a permanent effect in the political education of the masses, and as early as 1852 the Whigs abandoned their belief in the finality of the settlement of twenty years before. However, the Reform bills introduced in parliament were feeble and insincere; it was the movement of opinion among the unenfranchised, stimulated and interpreted by John Bright, which at length in 1866 gave the question reality and compelled the compliance of the legislature. Among the causes of this new interest the successive steps in the cheapening of newspapers must be reckoned. It is likely too that the incompetence shown in the earlier management of the Crimean war did something to discredit the ruling class. And at the end of the period the triumph of the Federal government in the American War of Secession, at a time when the United States was the only important democratic Power in the world, greatly excited the courage and hopes of English democrats; while the fortitude shown by the Lancashire operatives during the sufferings of the cotton famine convinced many of their countrymen that such men might be safely trusted with the vote.

The second Reform Act, passed in 1867 by the Conservatives under Disraeli, who had in the previous year with Whig assistance rejected Gladstone's milder proposals, was in its provisions, though not as a precedent, a far more drastic measure than the Act of 1832. That Act, while disfranchising the rottenest boroughs, had spared many hardly less insignificant; Bright asserted that even after 1832 more than half the House of Commons were returned by 180,000 voters. The new Act, by enfranchising householders and £10 lodgers in the towns, added to the electorate about a million voters, of whom the majority were now working men.

For the greater part of the period under review there was strange confusion, and not a little unreality, in the party system. On three occasions Tory statesmen remained in office, or resumed it, to pass measures of which their followers had long and resolutely opposed the principles; on a fourth occasion the Duke of Wellington was actually prepared to take office to pass the Whig Reform Bill. The Tories had the advantage that they could, while the Whigs could not, bring out the Duke on occasion to ensure the compliance of the Lords. Even more than by the hostility of the Lords, the Whigs were paralysed by the personal and political differences of their rival leaders. Palmerston cared nothing for Russell's Reform bills, and cheerfully applauded the rejection by the Lords of a money bill promoted by his own Cabinet. If Peel was a Tory Minister carrying Liberal measures, Palmerston was a Whig Minister obstructing them.

It was during this half-century that two of the great instruments of democracy first became recognized political forces in England : extra-parliamentary agitation and the daily press. There had been organized campaigns for Catholic Relief, for parliamentary reform, for the abolition of slavery, for cheap newspapers, for the repeal of the Union with Ireland, for a ten-hour factory day, for the repeal of the Poor Law and the Corn laws, for the Charter, and for household suffrage. Peel realized that the country could not be governed without regard to the opinion of the unenfranchised majority, and Disraeli accordingly inveighed against him as " the unconscious parent of political agitation." Meanwhile governments were changed as the result not, usually, of general elections, but of divisions in the House of Commons. In other words, while popular opinion was coming to play a decisive part, it had no recognized constitutional method of operation, not having been brought into organic and continuous relation with the House of Commons by a democratic suffrage and an effective party organization.

Meanwhile leading politicians—Canning and Brougham, perhaps, first—had learnt to recognize and exploit the immense power of the press. The primacy of *The Times* was unquestioned throughout the period. Delane, its editor from 1841 till 1877, was the confidant and the terror of ministers and ambassadors, and his leading articles could exert an influence that seems remarkable if one remembers that the circulation of the paper was only 40,000 in 1852, when it cost fivepence, and only 61,000 in the later sixties, when the price had been reduced to threepence. So narrow was still the circle of those whose opinion counted at a crisis.

Not the least interesting change in the period was the restoration of the prestige of the monarchy. No figure could have been less like the profligate, selfish, untruthful old Regent, or his stupid and unbalanced sailor brother, William, than the young queen who, inspired by her cousin-bridegroom, set herself and her servants a wonderful standard of integrity and hard work. She had strong prejudices, and she was often inconsiderate ; moreover her domestic advisers' ideas of monarchy were German rather than English. But she had common sense and knew when she must yield, and her suggestions were sometimes of great value to her Ministers, as when she prompted Derby in 1866 to a real settlement of the Reform question.

CHAPTER V

THE MACHINE OF GOVERNMENT

THE engine of government for whose control Disraeli and Gladstone fought at the general election of 1868 was a much more complicated and powerful instrument than Pitt had directed. The change had been forced by the needs of the national life despite the precepts of *laissez-faire*. It had begun even before the first Reform Act, but that convulsion mightily hastened the process. At home, new departments of State and new courts of law with new powers were created, and the police system, the Civil Service, and the machinery of local government were revolutionized. In the Empire new forms of polity were devised for India and the principal colonies.

In the character and methods of parliament no great changes were made, though that very English phrase, " His Majesty's Opposition," dates from 1826, and the first non-party Speaker of the Commons from 1839. Throughout the period there was no closure; a speech might last for five hours, and a debate for three weeks.

There were no official reports of speeches, but the newspapers gave them a great deal of space ; the courts decided in 1868 that the publisher of a fair report of what was said in parliament was not liable for defamation. An attempt by the government to introduce life peers into the House of Lords in 1856 was foiled by the Lords themselves. The relations between the two Houses rested after 1832 on a convention that the will of the Commons, if backed by the electorate, must eventually prevail ; but there was room foɪ much bickering. In finance the Commons had the whip hand ; Gladstone countered the Lords' rejection of a money bill in 1860 by sending up the whole of next year's proposed taxation in a single bill which the Lords could not alter and dared not reject.

To a stranger visiting England in 1815 the judicial system would have seemed as perverse and inexplicable as the system of representation. So long as Eldon, the Tory Chancellor, occupied the Woolsack, change was unthinkable. After 1830, under the influence of Bentham and common sense, procedure was greatly simplified. Most of the changes are too technical to mention, but some were on a larger scale. The most important feature was the decentralization of justice. In criminal cases the work done by stipendiary magistrates and Justices in Petty

Sessions was largely increased, and in 1846 parliament set up all over the country a system of County Courts—an old name for a new invention—to try civil cases in which no large sum was at stake. Then in 1857 a secular Court of Probate and Divorce was established; civil marriage had been made legal in 1836, and the new court was empowered to dissolve marriages. In 1833 the judicial work of the Privy Council, still the supreme authority in colonial and ecclesiastical appeals, was entrusted to a statutory committee of the Council.

Much greater changes were made in the organization of the Executive. The Cabinet itself remained small and handy; Grey's Reform Cabinet had thirteen members, Peel's model Cabinet of 1841 fourteen, Derby's of 1866 fifteen. But the number of first-class political offices increased. A fourth Secretary of State, for War, was appointed in 1854; a fifth, for India, in 1858. The Poor Law Commissioners of 1834 gave place to a Poor Law Board in 1847; a Board of Health was created in 1848, and a Minister for Education in 1856. The office of Controller and Auditor-General was established in 1866 for the purpose of putting the public finances under the protection of a permanent authority unaffected by party.

A foreign historian finds the aristocratic

and amateur character of English institutions well exemplified in the army. It was officered exclusively by the gentry, among whom commissions were bought and sold like seats in parliament. Advanced professional training was practically unknown. No contact existed between officers and other ranks; soldiers—who were enlisted for life—were drawn from the off-scourings of industry, if not of the gaols, and were treated as such alike by their military superiors and by the civilian population. By 1821 the strength of the Regular Army had been reduced to 100,000 men, of whom less than half were at home—no great force for quelling a revolution; even so democrats complained that the troops were cut off from sympathy with the common people by being quartered in barracks and not, as formerly, billeted in public-houses. When war broke out with Russia in 1854, there were 140,000 men serving with the Colours, half of them in India and the Colonies; there was no reserve except the Militia, recruited since 1852 by voluntary enlistment, and 10,000 pensioners. Forty years of peace had proved ruinous to military efficiency, and though the British force in the Crimea never exceeded 30,000 men the war showed up the incompetence and chaos of the administration. Even after the war the new Secretary of State and the

Commander-in-Chief co-existed as, to some extent, independent authorities. As a result of the Indian Mutiny the troops of the East India Company were absorbed in the Army, and the European garrison of India was fixed at 69,000 men. The institution of the Staff College in 1858 and of the Volunteer Force next year bore witness to a revived interest in military affairs. In the navy the most important changes were the transitions from sails to steam and from wooden to iron ships.

That the country was at peace after 1815 did not mean that the forces had nothing to do. Not only the regular troops, but also the Yeomanry, and to a less extent the Militia, were habitually used to maintain domestic order. To us such a state of things is hard to realize as normal, and we may therefore be inclined to overestimate the strength of revolutionary feeling in those years. But in the absence of a civil police force the government had no alternative, if it was not to fail in its primary duties. Yet the army, and still more the Yeomanry, composed largely of farmers' sons, was an exceedingly clumsy and provocative instrument to use for such a purpose. Peel therefore rendered a great service to the cause not only of efficient government but also of internal peace when he created a permanent police force for London in 1829.

Six years later the new system was made compulsory for all municipal boroughs, and by 1857 it had been applied to the whole of England. Attacked at first as un-English and tyrannical, it very soon justified itself in the eyes of sensible people, and it is not the least of the factors which increased the general welfare in the nineteenth century. In Ireland, where Peel had served his apprenticeship, the problem was far more difficult. There misery was chronic, and the population seemed to feel no interest in helping to suppress the outbreaks of violent crime. Whig and Tory Cabinets alike felt impelled to enact special laws to coerce this strange people to whom English institutions of government seemed uncongenial and unsuited.

The new police system could hardly have been applied to the English towns if the old borough corporations had remained in existence. Speaking generally, they were far too incompetent and corrupt to be entrusted with these, or indeed much less important, powers, and for some time it had been customary, when some new local service was needed, to create a special authority for the purpose. Often the work was done by private enterprise; companies were formed to maintain roads and light the streets. For the old oligarchical co-opted juntas, in which by ancient charters the government of most towns was vested, the Municipal Corporations Act of 1835 substituted councils elected by householders by a suffrage then regarded as democratic ; their judicial powers, however, passed not to the councils but to magistrates nominated by the Crown. The Councils were empowered to make bylaws and impose a rate. Apart from their responsibility to their electors, they were submitted to a triple check : like all subjects they were liable before the Courts for illegal acts and omissions ; their authority could be modified or withdrawn by parliament ; and many of their acts required approval by the Privy Council or a government department. Thus, while establishing a multitude of self-governing communities within the State, the Act at the same time added to the functions and powers of the Crown. Municipal self-government was established in Scotland, for the first time in her history, by the Burgh Act of 1833 ; Ireland did not obtain it till 1840, and then in no very democratic form. The English counties remained for half a century under the rule of the Justices in Quarter Sessions, who continued to combine judicial and administrative prerogatives.

In the case of the no less revolutionary measure passed by the Whigs the previous year, the New Poor Law of 1834, centralization and bureaucratic control were carried much further.

The Act transferred the administration of poor relief from the Justices to Boards of Guardians elected on a plutocratic system, dividing the country for the purpose into Unions. The Boards were bound hand and foot by the rules made by three Poor Law Commissioners in London, whose approval was needed for the appointment of local workhouse and relieving officials and who could even dismiss them when appointed. Such close central control was something the English town and village had not known for nearly two hundred years.

These two great measures of local government, the first fruits of the Reform Bill, are of further significance by reason of the manner of their conception. They were the outcome of two Royal Commissions, which heard evidence and produced voluminous reports. This procedure was often repeated : it was the beginning of scientific legislation, the legacy of old Jeremy Bentham, who ended his career of public usefulness in 1832, and we owe to it a mass of material invaluable for the social history of the time.

Several other important precedents were set in these years. The Factory Act of 1833 inaugurated that system of government inspection which alone made its successors effective. In the same year parliament made the first grant of public money for education, contributing

£20,000 towards the building of schools by voluntary effort. In 1834 the first annual grant-in-aid was made from the Exchequer to lighten the load of local taxation. In 1837 a Registration Act was passed, enjoining the registration of births and deaths and so for the first time making a scientific collection of vital statistics possible.

Town Councils and Boards of Guardians were not the only new local bodies created by parliament in the generation after the Reform Bill, nor were municipal boroughs and Poor Law Unions the only areas. The old custom of setting up new authorities to supply new services was continued, and Highway districts, Burial Board districts, Improvement Act districts, and Sanitary districts all emerged to confuse the administrative map. The most important of these were the last. Thanks to the tireless labours and irrepressible researches of Edwin Chadwick, the Benthamite secretary of the Poor Law Commissioners, the scandalous condition of the great towns with respect to housing, drainage, and water-supply was forced on the attention of the government. His report of 1842 on the sanitary condition of the labouring classes was followed by the report of a Royal Commission on the Health of Towns. At length in 1848, in the fear of cholera then prevalent, parliament established a General Board of Health with the duty of providing, where necessary, for local boards of health. In boroughs these were to be the Municipal Councils, and consequently the powers of the councils have been mainly derived from two sources, the parallel series of Municipal Corporation Acts and Public Health Acts. The General Board of Health created in 1848, which consisted in practice of Chadwick, Lord Ashley, and their medical adviser, Southwood Smith, was obstructed in its work by vested interests and came to an end in 1854, when Chadwick was dismissed. For all his efficiency, he was too much the inhuman official to get on with his countrymen, and he was odious to rich and poor alike. For the next seventeen years there was no central health authority with effective powers.

Alongside of the great general Acts, one very characteristic feature of English social legislation deserves notice. Individual boroughs had the right to promote private bills giving them powers not accorded to their fellows, and parliament itself sometimes passed " adoptive acts " or " model clauses " of which local authorities could take advantage if they liked. These practices, while fatal to uniformity, favoured the making of local experiments which might be useful in guiding the later course of general legislation.

We have seen how even in the heyday of *laissez-faire* practical needs led to an extension of State action in the supervision of factories, poor-relief, and sanitation. This tendency was not checked by the development of local responsibilities. On the contrary, it is noteworthy that every step in this development has increased the functions of the central departments and usually the number of their officials. In 1815 the Home Office managed with eighteen clerks. Such a staff obviously could not have coped with the new duties of supervising police, factories, and municipal government. The adoption of penny postage and the purchase of the telegraphs by the State multiplied the work of the Post Office, and railway regulation that of the Board of Trade. By 1853 the numbers of the Civil Service had risen to 16,000. The question how this army of officials should be recruited and organized, especially in the higher grades, had become one of supreme importance. There were the warnings of Byzantine and Napoleonic bureaucracy on the one hand, and on the other that of the American spoils system, proclaimed by Andrew Jackson just at the time when the first great blow against aristocratic predominance was struck in England. The solution invented in the fifties but not adopted till some time later ranks among the chief English contributions to the art of politics.

The way was pointed by the distinction drawn early in the eighteenth century between offices that were, and were not, tenable with a seat in parliament. Later, the disfranchisement of certain classes of officials was a further step towards the attainment of a non-political Civil Service. But though these rules might lessen the part played by the servants of the Crown in politics, they did not lessen the influence of politicians on the service of the Crown. In the first half of the nineteenth century the Patronage Secretary of the Treasury was besieged by members of both Houses asking for jobs for their relations or adherents, and the ceaseless flow of solicitations could make a Prime Minister's life almost unbearable. From one vice the system was free : owing to the strength of the English regard for vested interests officials were not liable, as in the United States, to lose their post when the opposite party came into power, and fixity of tenure made against time-serving if also against industry. Things were improved by the abolition of various sinecures and by the high standard of public duty exacted by Peel, but a report of 1853 laid a heavy indictment against the idlers and invalids drawing public money in the offices to which they had won their way by influence, but slightly checked in certain cases by perfunctory examinations.

The report mentioned had been prepared at Gladstone's request by Sir Stafford Northcote and Sir Charles Trevelyan ; it urged that candidates for all departments should be admitted on the results of a common competitive examination held under the auspices of a permanent board of examiners, and admitted in the first instance for a period of probation only. This principle, accepted for India in 1853, was considered too democratic for England by even a Liberal Whig like Russell, and, though a Civil Service Commission was set up in 1855 to hold examinations, open competition was not introduced for another fifteen years. But a mortal blow had been dealt to the old system. Henceforward the country was served by a staff of men who had received the best education of the day and who could be trusted to lay their talents at the disposal of whatever government might be in power. Their profession was made more attractive in 1859 by the institution of a pension system, and their ability combined with their permanence enabled some of them to sway the policy of their departments to a far greater extent than their transitory chiefs. Nowhere was this truer than in the Colonial Office, where between 1825 and 1868 four Permanent Heads saw twenty-six changes in the post of Secretary of State.

A problem in local government more important than that to which the Municipal Corporation Act offered a solution faced the rulers of the British Empire in the early nineteenth century. Among the many causes resulting in the secession of the thirteen American colonies the administrative difficulty was not the least: how to devise institutions which should maintain the imperial connection without jarring on the colonials' desire for self-government. The war left many dont's as its moral, but nothing constructive. The moral which found favour in England was that if you gave your colonies an inch they would take an ell. At any rate the new colonies acquired in the following period were not granted elected legislatures as had hitherto been the case. The new convict settlements in Australia could hardly expect them, and their form of government was purely autocratic until the twenties. In Cape Colony also, taken for its strategic value as a half-way house to India, the despotic rule of the Dutch régime was continued.

England's relations with her remaining North American colonies during the twenty-five years after Waterloo were no very good advertisement for the brand of representative government which they possessed. By 1840 rebellions had broken out in Upper and Lower Canada (Ontario and Quebec) and the British Cabinet had introduced a bill to suspend the constitution of Jamaica. Durham, Lord Grey's Radical son-in-law, who was sent out by the Melbourne government to deal with the situation in the Canadas, satisfied himself that their constitutions made friction inevitable. A Governor responsible to the Colonial Office and advised by a permanent Executive Council was matched against a locally elected assembly which enjoyed the power of the purse. Durham had the insight and courage to recommend that "responsible government" should be substituted for this diarchy, and to submit that the only action required was to instruct the Governor to choose for his ministers men who had the confidence of the local legislature. Herein he expressed the views of the "Colonial Reformers," a small group of able English Radicals, who alone in their generation realized something of the part which these outlying peoples and lands might play in British history. Durham's advice was not followed at once, but at length in the late forties his brother-in-law, Grey, at home and his son-in-law, Elgin, at Montreal co-operated to introduce into Canada the system of "responsible government" which he had imagined. It was a momentous decision, for the precedent then set was followed in the new colony of New Zealand in 1854, in Australia in 1856, in Cape Colony in 1872, and it has offered to the world new conceptions of colonial evolution and international relationships.

For Durham's principle led further than he foresaw. He had assumed that the control of certain matters, such as foreign policy and defence, trade, public lands and constitutional amendment, would remain with the mother-country and that the colony would acquiesce in " perfect subordination " on these points. It is well that he did so, for otherwise he and the Colonial Reformers might have found it difficult to answer those who asserted that this policy meant separation; undoubtedly its execution was helped by the pessimism of many who believed that separation was inevitable in any case, and that moreover, after the adoption of Free Trade, it did not much matter. Faith and indifference worked to the same end, and when the colonies, Canada leading the way, claimed to take over control of some of the reserved subjects, habit and theory alike in Downing Street made prolonged objection difficult. But it was no slight shock to both imperialists and Free Traders in England when in 1859 Canada insisted on framing her tariffs without regard to English opinion, so complete a negation was this of the old colonial relationship. Politicians and officials who had never crossed the Atlantic had not the insight to realize that a " close affection " could exist between England and her colonies without political or commercial dependence.

Eight years after the tariff claims had been made and admitted, confederation united the colonies on the North American mainland into a national whole as the Dominion of Canada. The right of amending their constitutions had long been accorded, subject to the royal veto, to British colonies individually, and in 1865 the Colonial Laws Validity Act made the concession general. Confederation was the result of Canadian initiative, completed and formalized by the imperial parliament, which enacted the constitution of the Dominion ; the same machinery was, and still is, required to amend it. The suggested title of " Kingdom of Canada " was dropped for fear of hurting republican feelings in the United States—a singular example of consideration for another Power ; its adoption would perhaps have been useful, as nationalist feeling grew in Canada, in asserting equality of status between the new nation and the mother-country. But in truth the relationship was determined not by words but by facts. A government ruling across America from ocean to ocean would obtain the status it desired as soon as it seriously claimed it.

In India the system established by Pitt, whereby a Governor-General, nominally the servant of the East India Company, ruled autocratically subject to the approval of a government department in London, lasted till 1858; in that year the Company, which had long lost its trading monopoly, dropped out, and the Governor-General became the Queen's Viceroy. Once political responsibilities had been accepted, it was impossible, in the absence of natural frontiers, not to extend them, and the British Empire grew like the Roman. Assam, Lower Burma, Sinde, the Punjab, the Central Provinces, and Oudh were annexed, but the policy of gradually absorbing the Native States in British India, as the direct line of their dynasties failed, was eventually abandoned. Early in the century the Indian administration, recruited from Englishmen of good education, acquired its tradition of justice and efficiency. As one of the results of the Mutiny, which was primarily an outbreak among the native troops in north-central India, the army was remodelled during the sixties. The proportion of British to Indian troops was raised from one-fifth to one-half, and all ranks of the artillery were henceforth to be British.

A century after Plassey the whole sub-conti-

H

nent lay quiet under British government or control. English had become the one language common to educated men throughout its vast territories ; education on western lines was introducing for good or ill western ideas of social and political relations ; but as yet there was no articulate protest against the military and political despotism which had given India a measure of peace and order unknown in her previous history.

CHAPTER VI

In the half-century after Waterloo Great Britain had to meet no threat to her national life or vital interests from a foreign Power, except possibly for a few weeks in 1831. For this enviable record she had to thank her fleet, her wealth, and the exhaustion of her neighbours. Sated with colonies and absorbed in industrial and commercial expansion, she never forgot, except at moments of transitory excitement, that her main interest was peace. But she had to decide what attitude to international affairs was most likely to preserve it.

The periods of greatest moment in British foreign relations during this half-century are three. The first is the period between 1815 and 1833, when difficulties springing from the Vienna settlement raised the whole question of the nature of the responsibilities falling on the Great Powers and of the principles of international co-operation. The second is the period of the Crimean war, involving the Eastern question and the principle of the balance of power. The third, from 1859 onwards, was dominated by the great struggles for national unity in Europe and America. Great Britain emerged from the half-century without becoming involved in more than one major war, but she fought several on a small scale in Asia, and at the close she had lost her old position of confident security.

Lord Castlereagh was the least insular of British Foreign Secretaries. Convinced that nothing but the close co-operation between the Great Powers which had won the peace could possibly maintain it, he had committed his country to resume hostilities along with Austria, Prussia, and Russia should France invade her neighbours' territory or accept a Bonaparte restoration; England was moreover bound to "concert measures" with the three Powers and with the King of France should a revolutionary rising in France endanger the general peace. The treaty of alliance further contained one novel provision—for periodical meetings of the Allied sovereigns or their ministers for the purpose of consulting as to their common interests and the means of preserving peace. This was Castlereagh's own peculiar contribution to the practice of diplomacy. He believed not only that the common interests of the States of Europe were large and important enough to be made the foundation of a common policy, but that such personal contact as he had himself established with their leading statesmen would be an invaluable means of forming and following it. " It really appears to me," he said, " to be a new discovery in the European Government, at once extinguishing the cobwebs with which diplomacy obscures the horizon, bringing the whole bearing of the system into its true light, and giving to the counsels of the Great Powers the efficiency and almost the simplicity of a single State."

But it soon appeared that the most powerful of the Continental potentates had ideas differing widely from Castlereagh's as to the uses that might be made of the new solidarity. The Tsar Alexander proposed that each State should guarantee not only the territory but the existing form of government of its neighbours ; he wished to use the alliance to stamp out any disturbance of the existing order from without or from within. The question soon became practical. Only a few years after the peace a fresh era of revolution began in southern Europe. The Tsar and Metternich, the Austrian Chancellor, demanded collective intervention. Castlereagh disliked revolutions as much as anyone, but he had never intended that his country should play the policeman or the schoolmaster. Indeed parliamentary England could hardly teach the

same constitutional lesson as despotic Austria
or Russia. In his view, interference could only
be warranted if a revolution caused " direct and
imminent danger " to another State. " We shall
be found in our place," he wrote in a historic
state paper, " when actual danger menaces the
System of Europe, but this country cannot, and
will not, act upon abstract and speculative
Principles of Precaution." Consequently from
1818 onwards Castlereagh opposed intervention,
whether in support of rebels or of their legitimate
sovereign ; but he could move with events,
and in the case of the revolted Spanish colonies
in South America, where British commercial
interests were closely affected, he advanced with
conservative reluctance from mere refusal to
join in their forcible suppression, to recognizing
them as commercial, if not yet as political, units.

It is in North America, however, that Castlereagh's wisdom won its most lasting success.
Resolved to restore friendly relations between
the British Empire and the United States after
the futile war of 1812–14, he and President
Monroe forestalled future bickerings by agreeing
not to maintain rival navies on the Great Lakes.
The extension of this policy of common sense to
land forces also has made the undefended
Canadian frontier an example to the world.

Castlereagh's tragic death in 1822 closed an

epoch in the history of British foreign relations. His policy, indeed, was maintained and developed by his more dashing successor; it was the point of view which had changed. He said himself: "No one after me understands the affairs of the Continent." Certainly no one had the European mind; for while Castlereagh regretted every occasion when he was unable to work with the Alliance, it was Canning's dearest wish to break it up. Castlereagh had made a great attempt to use the fleeting opportunity of the peace to anchor his country in the habit of European co-operation. He failed, because he was ahead of public opinion and of the facts. The facts were against him, because there was in truth little common ground between England and the eastern monarchies; public opinion was against him, because it knew little of foreign countries, and disliked what it knew, and also because he himself did nothing to instruct and mould it. Here lay the difference between him and his successor.

Castlereagh, the great noble, unrivalled in knowledge and experience, could command the confidence of the High Tories in the Cabinet and the House of Commons. Canning, the new man, in office only because his genius made him indispensable, had no such support; for help against the intrigues of the Court and his colleagues he looked to public opinion, meaning thereby the opinion of the professional and business men who counted for so much in the new liberal England. The instrument with which he rallied them was publicity ; he addressed them, in and out of the House, with a superb eloquence, and he published dispatches soon after they were written. The effect was astonishing ; the patriotism of the country sprang to his side, and foreign statesmen took note of it.

As Castlereagh was less reactionary than his reputation, so perhaps Canning was less advanced. He had no love for rebels, nor for republics, and he hated the Alliance not because it was despotic but because it was meddlesome and countered British interests. " For ' Alliance,' read ' England,' " he wrote, " and you have the clue of my policy." So strong a nationalist was not likely to interpret non-intervention as mere quiescence. The intervention he disliked was the collective intervention of the Alliance in domestic matters. He was willing to intervene to prevent such intervention, by force, if necessary, where British interests were involved, and where naval action could be effective, as in the case of the South American colonies. In the negotiations tending towards the recognition of these colonies as independent nations, Canning tried to secure the co-operation of the United

States—a Power whose society was not then usually courted by European statesmen; in this he failed, and his policy of keeping the southern continent open to British influence received something of a jar from the pronouncement of the Monroe doctrine; but none the less the Monroe doctrine could hardly have been proclaimed but for the knowledge in Washington that Canning was prepared to use the British fleet to prevent French interference in South America. Canning's greatest feat, however, was in Europe: by taking skilful advantage of a breach between the Tsar and Metternich he contrived finally to break up the syndicate of autocrats miscalled the Holy Alliance, and to substitute for it the understanding between Great Britain, Russia and France which secured Greece her independence. Possibly Canning was too ready to contemplate war as a diplomatic weapon, and he set a dangerous example to his pupil and eventual successor, Palmerston. Fortunately for peace, England was not in a position to send troops abroad in any numbers, and no foreign Power was inclined to challenge her navy.

The effect of Canning's statesmanship was seen in 1830, three years after his death, when the last legitimist king of France was dethroned by the mob, and shortly afterwards the Belgians

rose in revolt against their Dutch king. An
outbreak of revolutionary principles in France,
leading directly to a breach of the territorial
settlement of Vienna ; what clearer case could
Alexander have desired for the intervention of
the Alliance ? But its prestige was now shattered, and the atmosphere had changed. The
Tory Ministers, Wellington and Aberdeen, though
partners and heirs of the Castlereagh tradition,
resolved at once to recognize the new bourgeois
King of the French. Only a few months later
they were succeeded by Grey and Palmerston,
who had no objection to the new dynasty. All
their goodwill, however, was needed to keep the
peace in the matter of the Low Countries, then
as always considered a vital one by British
statesmen. The separation of Belgium from
Holland was accepted as inevitable by a Conference of the Powers, though it was the undoing
of the work of 1815 ; but the British government was resolved, even at the cost of war,
not to allow such an extension of French influence in Belgium as would result either from
the accession to the new throne of a French
prince or from an indefinite occupation of the
country by French troops. Perhaps no threat
to British interests in the half-century after
Waterloo was taken more seriously than this ;
but the real danger of war was slight, since it

was clearly as much as King Louis Philippe's throne was worth to fall foul of his only powerful friend. By 1833 the question of the Netherlands was virtually settled, though it was not till six years later that the final treaties were signed providing for the perpetual neutrality of Belgium under the guarantee of the signatory Powers, including Great Britain, France, and Prussia.

Throughout the nineteenth century British opinion wavered as to whether France or Russia, the known or the unknown rival, was the more dangerous. France was still " the hereditary enemy," and from time to time incidents occurred causing mutual irritation, distrust, and even thoughts of war; yet in spite of such recurrent crises the two western Liberal Powers were drawn together by those common elements of their political and social life which separated them from the eastern autocracies. This disposition to co-operate, fostered in the forties by the pacific statesmanship of Aberdeen, survived the fall of Louis Philippe in the commotions of 1848 and the *coup d'état* by which Louis Napoleon made himself supreme three years later. In 1854 it brought the two Powers into the field together as the protectors of decadent Turkey against Russia.

Curiously enough, on the last occasion when the affairs of Turkey had been prominent, in

the matter of Syria in 1840, the British and the
French policies had been sharply opposed, and
England had been in measurable distance of
fighting France as the ally of Russia. But
now Russia was the bugbear. Western nationalists feared her vast and always increasing
resources in territory and men ; western Liberals
detested her institutions and her aggressiveness.
To both it was intolerable that she should pose
as a kind of suzerain of the Turkish Empire
with vague privileges of interference. Such
feelings, loudly and at length menacingly expressed in the circles that counted politically,
drove a hesitating British Cabinet into war,
although the Tsar had accepted a formula of
settlement proposed to him by Great Britain
and the three other Powers, and although the
Court, the Prime Minister, and the leaders of
the Manchester School worked desperately for
peace. But the nation believed with Palmerston
and Stratford Canning, the masterful ambassador
at Constantinople, that the " imperial bully "
needed a lesson. So 25,000 lives and some
seventy million pounds—impressive totals in
those days—were spent in combating dangers of
very doubtful reality. Even when victory came
it imposed nothing but a temporary check on
Russian policy, and the guarantee of Turkish
territory and independence given by the Powers

and secretly confirmed by Great Britain, France and Austria was of no more lasting importance.

The significance of the Crimean muddle in English history is of another kind. It was the first time that the new force of the middle classes' interest in politics, as expressed in public meetings and the press, had diverted the foreign policy of a government. It was the last time that a British ambassador, unhampered by the telegraph, could carry on a policy of his own at a foreign court. It demonstrated, moreover, that a line of action zig-zagging between two policies might be more fatal than action in accordance with either. For it was open to Palmerston, who succeeded to the direction of the war, to maintain that had his " firm policy " been consistently followed the Tsar would never have given the Turks the provocation they desired and that war would have been averted.

Palmerston's firmness had succeeded with France in 1831 and 1840, and with Russia, over the protection of the Hungarian refugees, in 1849. Against weaker antagonists it might seem less heroic. He used the fleet in a sordid cause to coerce Greece in 1850. He fought China in 1839–41 to secure a higher status for the British representative and in defence of British traders, but the affair savoured unpleasantly of opium; Hong Kong, then a desert island, was the prize of victory. He fought China again in 1857–60, as the result of an incident in which his country was clearly in the wrong, and this time forced her to admit a British ambassador to her capital. Having been defeated in the House of Commons on the Chinese issue, he appealed to the electorate and was triumphantly returned to power; in the following year he was again defeated—by a curious irony—for having been too conciliatory to the French Emperor. He had taught his countrymen to take no lowly view of British prestige.

Palmerston subscribed to the doctrine of non-intervention held by Castlereagh and Canning, when it was a matter of intervening by force in matters not directly affecting British interests; but he held that his country was entitled, and required by her position as a Great Power, to use her strength abroad as " the champion of justice and right, pursuing that course with moderation and prudence, not becoming the Quixote of the world, but giving the weight of her moral sanction and support wherever she thinks that justice is, and wherever she thinks that wrong has been done." Many even of the Manchester School applauded him when, as the spokesman of Liberal England, he denounced cruelty and oppression in foreign countries.

They parted company with him when he backed his opinions with the British fleet. But Palmerston trusted his own judgment, believing that a show of force was often the surest way to peace. It was a risky policy, but Palmerston was a sportsman and enjoyed sailing close to the wind. Cobden, on the other hand, advocated arbitration and disarmament, and hoped that war would disappear with the advent of universal Free Trade; in fact he did much to dispel a war scare in 1860, when Palmerston thought only of iron-clads, forts, and volunteers, by negotiating a commercial treaty with the French Emperor. But besides foreigners and internationalists, Palmerston's outbursts infuriated his very English queen—as a queen, however, not as an Englishwoman. She was incensed at his reflections on other sovereigns and his casual neglect of her own prerogatives. She was no cipher in foreign affairs, and for a blazing indiscretion in 1851 she secured his dismissal.

During the third critical period, from 1859 onwards, Palmerston was Prime Minister, and Russell, his former chief, Foreign Secretary. The two old men were confronted by a succession of crises in which nationality was the motive force. Whether any recognized machinery of international conciliation could have kept the peace is highly doubtful. The British Foreign

Office could do nothing but labour to prevent a general war, and here it was successful.

In 1859, though it was clear that peace could not be preserved in view of the conflicting wills of France, Austria, and Sardinia, Britain tried hard to preserve it, and declared that she would remain neutral herself. But the character of the British neutrality was all-important. This depended on the play of party politics at Westminster; the Conservatives were much less favourably inclined to the Italian patriots than were their Whig-Liberal opponents who succeeded them in June. Palmerston and Russell, though friends of Italian liberty, only gradually became converted, by the march of events and their distrust of Napoleon III, to the programme of Italian unity. Suspicion of France was indeed the dominant factor with them throughout. By the summer of 1860 their conversion was a fact, and in October Russell caused consternation in the Courts of Europe, including his own, by publicly applauding the action of Sardinia in invading the Neapolitan and Papal dominions in support of the revolutionary parties. The resentment aroused by this dispatch was the only price, but it was not an insignificant one, which England had to pay for the smiles of Italy.

Analogies are usually dangerous, particularly

in politics, and yet more particularly in questions of nationality, of which no objective definition has yet been discovered. It was a bad mistake when the British upper classes saw in the secession of the southern States of the American Union merely the attempt at national self-expression of an aristocratic community whose manners they liked and whose cotton they found useful. They long failed to see that the spirit of nationality was really fighting in the ranks of the North ; that no nation could permanently remain " half slave and half free," and that the United States had become a nation which could not permit the secession of a part of itself. The mistake was excused by the fact that Seward, the Federal Secretary of State, kept declaring that the struggle had nothing to do with slavery ; but it was not made by the working classes and the Radicals, who by personal and political sympathy were in closer touch with American life.

The distrust of Great Britain in the United States, kindled by two wars, had been kept alive since the Treaty of Ghent in 1814 by a series of incidents, mostly unimportant in themselves, springing in the main from two facts—that a British colony was the United States' principal neighbour and that, in their attempts to suppress slave-trading, British men-of-war often interfered with United States ships. Various disputes, however, had been settled without war—notably that of 1846 concerning the Canadian frontier west of the Rockies—and relations between the two countries were perhaps friendlier than ever before when the election of Abraham Lincoln as President raised the Secession issue in 1860.

The major question that arose between Lincoln's government and Palmerston's was whether Great Britain would recognize the Confederate South as an independent State ; as a belligerent she was bound to recognize it after the North had declared a blockade of the Southern ports. The official view in England from the beginning had been that the South would certainly win its independence ; this view was confirmed by the military successes of the South in the first phase of the war. Consequently in the autumn of 1862 the desire to stop further bloodshed, England's strong interest in ending the blockade, and the usual fears of French intrigues combined to make the government think seriously of recognizing the independence of the South. But this grave danger to the future relations of the British Empire and the United States passed ; the turn of the tide of war in the summer of 1863 finally destroyed it, and before then Lincoln's proclamation identifying the cause of the

North with the abolition of slavery had brought the true issue home to the British people.

The most serious risks of war between the two countries in these momentous years sprang from two minor disputes, known to history by the names of two ships. In the *Trent* case a Federal naval officer had forcibly removed two Confederate envoys from a British ship; the other controversy arose out of Russell's negligence in allowing the *Alabama* and other ships to be built in British yards for the use of the Confederates. Far more serious than these details was the feeling widespread in the Northern States that at the crisis of their destiny the British government and people had shown them no sympathy. They failed to realize how little was known in England of American facts, and that the active supporters of the South were a small minority.

In Italy, despite England's determination not to go to war and her reluctance to play the game of the French Emperor, circumstances had produced conditions acceptable to the majority of the British people. In the cases of Poland and Slesvig it was not so fortunate. Russell's action —if action it can be called—in support of the revolted Poles in 1863 showed a complete failure to adapt behaviour to realities. His strong-worded protests to Russia, which he had no intention of supporting by force, exasperated the Tsar, fatally encouraged the Poles, and disinclined Napoleon III, who much to his own disadvantage had been induced to join in them, from any further co-operation with Great Britain. His disinclination was confirmed by Russell's peremptory refusal to support the ill-timed French proposal for a general Congress to consider the revision of the treaties of 1815.

The distrust thus accentuated between England and France, and between them both and Russia, ruined any chance there might have been of preventing the aggression of Prussia and Austria against Denmark in the beginning of 1864. The details of the Slesvig-Holstein affair are among the most complicated in modern history, but the main issue is fairly simple. The two German Powers, borne by the rising tide of German nationalism, early in 1864 invaded the duchy of Slesvig, which, like Holstein, was part of the dominions of the King of Denmark but, unlike Holstein, was not part of the German Confederation. In so acting they violated the Treaty of London which they both had signed in 1852. Having crushed the Danish resistance, they forced the king to surrender the two duchies, including a large Danish population in Slesvig. Disagreement as to the division of these ill-gotten spoils was the immediate cause of the

Prusso-Austrian war of 1866, by which Austria was expelled from Germany and the North German Confederation was formed under the hegemony of Prussia. The Danish government had shown a disregard of its obligations and a stupid obstinacy, but Palmerston and Russell took the view, which was shared by the bulk of British opinion, though not by the Queen, that the German Powers were flagrantly in the wrong. Palmerston rashly declared in parliament in July 1863 that Denmark would not stand alone if she were the victim of aggression, and Russell worked hard to secure joint intervention by Great Britain, France, and Russia. The Tsar, however, was now on terms of close friendship with Prussia, and Napoleon had no confidence in England after the events of 1863. Armed action by Great Britain alone was considered, but judged useless, so Bismarck was able to carry through unhindered the first of the wars by which he built up the German Empire. The case was quite different from the Italian ; in the wars of Italian unity there was no parallel to the forcible incorporation of the Slesvig Danes in a foreign State against their will. It was a case, if ever there was one, for the collective intervention of the Concert of Europe, and British statesmanship is to be blamed rather for having by clumsy diplomacy made such intervention impossible than for failure to take up arms alone. The results were momentous; if Austria was, paradoxically, the first to suffer, the turn of Russia, France, and Great Britain came exactly fifty years after 1864, when Prussia invaded the territory of another small Power in violation of another treaty.

CHAPTER VII

THE MIND OF THE SIXTIES

THE sixties of last century saw no such spectacular changes in the British islands as the making of united Italy and Germany, or as the emancipation of the Russian serfs, or as the Civil War and abolition of slavery in North America, or as the opening of Japan; but they were nevertheless a transitional period of profound importance in the history of thought as well as of politics. Politically, Britain was the leading world-power, indeed the only one; but more than this, she was the creator of a new type of civilization which the whole western world was hastening to adopt. Though Whig noblemen might still represent her in Downing Street and on the Treasury Bench, it was the industrial forces which were the secret of her greatness and determined the line of her advance. The amazing rate of industrial progress, due to the concentration of capital and the new technology, gave the colour to men's thoughts and encouraged them to assume progress as the law of life in every sphere. It was a sanguine age, conscious of great achievements and confident of greater to come. It was no doubt too prone to measure achievement by material success. Whatever did not pay was despised, and the æsthetic side of life was shamefully neglected : except in literature, artistic attainment was very mediocre. But mid-Victorian complacency might find excuses not only in the fields of manufacture and commerce : in the last year of the fifties appeared *Adam Bede* and *Richard Feverel*, Mill's *Liberty* and the *Origin of Species*, and it was a healthy feature of the age that it produced such outspoken critics as Dickens and Carlyle, Ruskin and Matthew Arnold, along with its admirers like Macaulay and Tennyson. As man cannot live by business alone, so it is not economic and political facts only which shape his thought. What other influences had moulded, and were moulding, the mind of the sixties ? What were the established ideas, and by what ideas were they challenged ?

In the first place, there was Christianity. To say nothing of Scotland with her parish schools and democratic kirk, or of Ireland with her intense religious differences, England was a Christian country in the sixties in a way she had not been forty years earlier. The Nonconformist bodies had made great progress, and the established Church was served in the country parishes, and even in the industrial districts, by clergymen very different from the curates described by Jane Austen and Charlotte Brontë. The remedying of other abuses had quelled the storm of hostility directed against the Church and Christianity generally about the time of the Reform Bill. The middle period of Victoria's reign was a Bible-reading, church-going, Sunday-keeping age; people hung texts in their bedrooms and subscribed to missions. In fashionable society the change was very remarkable. The pagan laxity of the Regency, inherited from the eighteenth century, had yielded to the tide of the Evangelical revival, swelling up from lowlier levels and strengthened by the awful warning from France. Wilberforce, more than any other man, had been responsible for the change of tone, and his mantle had fallen on Shaftesbury. The places of education had been affected. As Simeon and Maurice after him had turned minds to religion at Cambridge, so Thomas Arnold and other head-masters in his wake had done much to Christianize the Public Schools. The ideal of a Christian gentleman was set up beside that of a gentleman and a scholar. King's College had been founded in London as a Christian makeweight to its Gower Street rival. Christian motives played a direct and powerful part in the humanitarian activities which abolished slavery, flogging, and duelling, which regulated conditions in factories and asylums, and which were beginning to work for the protection of animals. The first socialist movement to win a name in English history was the Christian Socialism of Maurice and Kingsley. Tennyson's outlook was definitely Christian, and he was the representative poet of the age.

English Christianity was still emphatically Protestant. Russell's tirade against " Papal Aggression " in 1850 won immediate popularity, and it must have seemed inconceivable that the laity could ever forget the fires of Smithfield. But Protestantism was challenged, and in the minds of the clergy with growing insistence, by the new-old doctrines regarding the meaning of a church, of tradition, of sacraments, and of a priesthood, proclaimed from Oxford a generation before. High Churchmanship had come to mean something larger than scorn of Dissenters. Convocation had begun to meet again, and the first Lambeth Conference had been convoked. From time to time ritualistic Anglican priests chafed indignantly at the ecclesiastical jurisdiction of the Privy Council, and there were some in England, as there had been many in Scotland twenty years earlier, who wondered if an estab-

lished church could ever maintain its freedom
and its self-respect. It was twenty years since
Newman had left the Anglican communion, and
now he had just explained to the world in
matchless prose the process of his conversion.
Manning was an archbishop of the Roman
Church.

It was not from the Catholic side only that
Evangelical orthodoxy was challenged. The
French ideas which had sapped Eldonian Toryism were threatening religious dogma too. The
Benthamites who joined with the " Saints " in
their humanitarian crusades were largely agnos-
tics, and atheism was pungently preached to the
London artisans of the thirties. A generation
later, many of the most eminent minds, such
as John Stuart Mill, Herbert Spencer, George
Eliot, George Meredith, were frankly not Christian, and both German scholarship and physical
science were adding to the ranks of their followers. One recruit, John Morley, reminds us
that " the favourite poet of the time sang that
there was more faith in honest doubt than in
half your creeds, and awoke a long train of
uneasy thoughts by the sombre reminder that
Nature with ravin is red in tooth and claw."
Other thoughtful men, whose faith in Christianity survived such trials, were not afraid to
apply criticism, historical or ethical, to the inter-

pretation of the Bible, and to question such
doctrines as those of everlasting punishment
and a personal devil, which the current orthodoxy maintained. Persecuted in the fifties, they
soon made good their position in the Church ;
but had it not been subject to the control of the
State, they would doubtless have been expelled.

If Christianity was one established influence,
assuredly Liberalism was another. To most
Continental Catholics, as to Newman, the two
forces were as incompatible as light and darkness. But in England there was Nonconformity
to bridge the gap, and by a miracle the leader
of the new Liberal party was an enthusiastic
High Churchman, more deeply interested in
theology than in politics. English Liberalism
was broad enough to cover them both ; indeed,
it was not so much the creed of a party as a
habit of mind. It was established, not only in
the narrow sense that between 1846 and 1874
no Conservative ministry held office for much
more than a year on end, but in the sense that
nearly all thinkers and writers of eminence paid
homage to its principles.

Its principles were many. Its root, said John
Morley, is " respect for the dignity and worth
of the individual." Such respect cannot pre-
sume to dictate what good he is to seek, nor
how ; so it must promote the cult of liberty

for the sake of character—liberty to know, to
criticize, to disbelieve, to bargain, to learn by
one's own experience.   Hence Liberals accepted
the doctrines of *laissez-faire* in church and
market.   If Tennyson was the poet of the age,
its prophet laureate was Mill, Bentham's spiritual
grandson.   Mill's treatise *On Liberty* was hailed
as the final oracle of truth.   In it he sought to
trace a line between those actions of a person
which do, and those which do not, affect others
beside himself, and he argued that he is account-
able to society only for the first.   He followed
the line he had traced so far as to withhold from
parents the liberty not to educate their children,
and from intending parents the liberty to marry
if they lacked the means to support a family.
He was not an individualist of the extreme type
of Herbert Spencer, who regarded the State as
the enemy of man.   Indeed, as time passed,
Mill became more and more convinced that
liberty was not secured by the scramble of
capitalistic industry; he came to approve
greater and greater interferences with rights of
property, and at length admitted the principle
that property should be distributed " by concert
on an acknowledged principle of justice."   Thus
his teaching provided a bridge over which his
followers might march out of the dry land of
Benthamite individualism into climes where the

social group was taken as the unit. Many
different currents of thought were moving, or
would soon be moving, in this direction. There
were the Tories interested in history, who conceived the nation as composed of estates, and
the High Churchmen who saw individual men
as members of one spiritual Body. There were
the Oxford students of German metaphysics,
who were developing into a philosophy Rous-
seau's belief in a General Will and the sanctity
of a sovereign whole. There were the students
of German administration, who blushed as
Englishmen to observe how far the Prussian
State excelled their own in paternal efficiency.
From all these directions the individualist creed
was challenged ; but in the meantime it was an
inspiration of living force.

" Respect for the dignity and worth of the
individual " was not compatible with personal
slavery, and Liberals with some striking exceptions ranged themselves on the side of the
Federals in the American Civil War. In politics
the principle pointed to government by discussion, and Liberals assumed, despite Prussia's
chilling example, that every State in the front
rank would adopt representative institutions
after either the British or the American model.
On the subject of the parliamentary franchise,
it was difficult for Liberals to exclude any

responsible adult. Mill in 1861 accepted the principle of universal suffrage, with the provision that educated people should have extra votes, while Gladstone scandalized Conservatives and Whigs three years later by asserting similar doctrine on grounds of moral right.

When most men spoke of universal adult suffrage, they ignored women. Mill meant what he said. To him and a few others the Liberal principle could know no limit of sex, and in spheres wider than politics it was clear to them that the conventions of the age, as of preceding ages, implied a miserably inadequate recognition of the dignity and worth of the individual woman. The modern movement for her " emancipation," with its incalculable potentialities, began in the fifties and sixties of last century. The lives of thousands of working women had been already transformed by the industrial revolution, which made them primarily wage-earners rather than housekeepers; what working women needed was not emancipation so much as protection. We have seen that the first law regulating women's employment was the Mines Act of 1842; the flogging of women had been forbidden by the humanitarian legislation of the twenties. Henceforward the differential treatment of women in industry was accepted by all but the most doctrinaire feminists. But the industrial revolution, which enlarged the occupations open to working women, narrowed the lives of women of the middle classes. Much of the work of housekeeping and preparing food was made superfluous by the improvements in transport. An ordinary middle-class woman who remained unmarried was doomed to a round of monotonous idleness at home ; if driven to earn her living, she was likely to starve, for she had no choice but to join the overcrowded ruck of governesses or needlewomen. Girls' schools were a farce, and aimed at turning out accomplished, not educated, women. To be called " strongminded " was the cruellest of reproaches, and the very bales of unnecessary clothing in which women swathed themselves showed that they were destined for an inert and sedentary life. If a girl married, unless she belonged to the wealthy classes the law handed over any property she might possess to her husband, and until 1857 only wealth could buy a divorce if the marriage ended in disaster. Wives were expected to obey their lords and masters.

The revolt against this state of things was led by a few ladies of gentle demeanour but firm purpose, born round about the year 1830. Florence Nightingale created a new profession for her sex, and proved before the eyes of all Europe that a woman could face horrors without swooning and act more efficiently than men.   Barbara Bodichon, Emily Davies, and the two Garrett sisters, worked as pioneers, with eventual success, for the admission of women to university education, to the medical profession, and to the parliamentary suffrage.   Josephine Butler faced intense social disapproval in her crusade for the redress of the wrongs done them by unjust discrimination in moral questions.   The stars of literature in their courses fought on these women's side. The Amelia Sedleys were sinking, and though the radiance of Clara Middleton and Diana Merion was still below the horizon, Rose Jocelyn had dawned, while Romola and her creator blazed high in heaven.   The poets were with them too.   Tennyson, in *The Princess*, had opened the whole question twenty years before, and in the last years of the sixties Browning, a poet's husband, portrayed Pompilia Franceschini.   Nor did the movement disdain lowlier help ; by the seventies women in several trades had their own unions, and later even lawn tennis and bicycles played their part.

The same respect for individuality led Liberals to sympathize with the nationalism of their day, especially when it meant casting off the yoke of an alien autocrat.   The cause which forty years before had inspired Byron and Shelley now moved Browning, Meredith, and Swinburne.

The presence of illustrious exiles like Mazzini and Hugo kept Englishmen alive to foreign interests and preached the unity of Liberalism. There was also present in London in these years a Prussian Jew named Marx, usually deep in the British Museum but not uninterested in practical affairs, as he proved in 1864 by writing an address for the first meeting of the International Working Men's Association, better known as the First International. However, the internationalism characteristic of the period was not proletarian but commercial, and its prophet was not Marx but Cobden. Not that Cobden pursued peace for the sake of commerce ; on the contrary Free Trade was chiefly precious to him as " breaking down the barriers that separate nations." Free Trade was one means, but only one ; he worked also for the refusal of loans to militaristic powers, for arbitration treaties, and for the reduction of armaments. Cobden's hopes lay in the maximum of economic, and the minimum of political, contact between nations. Non-intervention in foreign politics was the natural companion of the doctrine that forbade interference with the life of the individual.

But against this habit of tolerance, this confidence in unregulated human character, a reaction was preparing. Carlyle had long been preaching the complementary virtues of discipline and drive, and from 1862 onwards his principles were being practised in Prussia by the spiritual descendant of his hero Frederick. In 1873, the year of Mill's death, Sir James Fitzjames Stephen replied in the name of authority and tradition to the theory which Mill had done so much to enthrone in the sixties.

Besides its Christianity and its Liberalism, the mind of the age was swayed by a force so variously manifested that it is hard to find a common name for its expressions, though their common connection with the Romantic revival gives them a certain historical unity. Mid-Victorian Liberalism adored reason. The elusive influence which now concerns us was a matter not of reason but of emotion; it was perhaps the expression of a yearning to escape from the drab realm of the expected and pursue the adventurous paths where wonder has her home. Typical of it are the elements of interest in nature and in the past which occur in Scott, Coleridge, and Wordsworth, in Keats, Shelley, and Byron; an interest often irradiated with that glamour of simple enthusiasm which the previous century abhorred. Culture was still based on the Greek and Latin classics, but it was the classics romanticized, as Turner and Keats had treated them; this influence appears in the paintings and sculpture of Watts, in

Tennyson's *Ulysses* and *Oenone*, in Swinburne's *Atalanta*, Browning's *Balaustion* and Matthew Arnold's *Thyrsis*. Nor had the romantic interest in the Middle Ages faded. The Oxford Movement had strengthened it; the architecture of the day paid it homage; it affected the forms of polite conversation. It came out strongly in Tennyson's Arthurian poems, in Ruskin, and in the whole Pre-Raphaelite movement, while the scholarship of Stubbs, Freeman, and J. R. Green was piercing the darkness in which medieval history had lain hidden.

Not only were the poets of nature read and admired, but the desire for knowledge of her wildness at first hand was expressing itself in new ways. Livingstone and Stanley explored central Africa, and the founding of the Alpine Club in 1858 gave recognition to a new enterprise to which some of the ablest living Englishmen had introduced the Continent. The Victorian ideal embraced healthy bodily vigour, and Meredith was truly Victorian when he insisted that sense, brain and spirit must interact harmoniously to produce the full life. Horse-racing and fox-hunting had long been English institutions, in which all classes were interested, and cricket appears to have in some degree succeeded to the place of prize-fighting. As more and more of the population became town-dwellers, outdoor recreation became more than ever desirable. Fresh forms of exercise, such as football, obtained rank as institutions. Meanwhile, the country-side was receding before the encroachment of slums and suburbs. Years before, Tennyson had commended squires who on occasion threw their grounds open to the neighbourhood ; now cheap travelling made seaside excursions possible for working people, and piers and esplanades fed their imaginations with visions of romance.

Lastly we must take account of the great and growing influence of natural science. The achievements of applied science working as capital's ally are events in economic and political history ; we are here concerned with the force exercised by the development of science on the mind of the period. Science itself was nothing new ; it had flourished in England for two hundred years. What was new was the organization ; what Professor Whitehead has called the " process of disciplined attack upon one difficulty after another." " The greatest invention of the nineteenth century was the invention of the method of invention." Its importance was not confined to any one group of studies ; in economics and history, in the criticism of classical and theological texts, a new method was elaborated. New also was the public interest in the actual inventions, an interest due not only to their commercial value but to the vast expansion of controlled power which they represented; the first locomotives made a profound impression on the imagination. Thus the March of Mind, so much bragged of in the twenties and thirties, was turned in a scientific direction, and, when the Schoolmaster walked abroad, alike in the universities and in Mechanics' Institutes scientific instruction was asked of him at the turn of the century. The Natural Science Tripos was instituted at Cambridge in 1850, and in the sixties science was being taught in the Public Schools. The creation of teaching posts in its turn promoted scientific research, by making it less generally dependent on the possession of a private income, such as Darwin had enjoyed.

To the man in the street science meant steam-engines and the telegraph, chloroform and anti-septics; to the thinker it meant new conceptions of the nature of the universe. The main work of John Dalton, Thomas Young, and Humphry Davy in chemistry, physics, and electro-magnetism was done before 1815; Faraday was in his prime in the thirties and forties, Thomson (Lord Kelvin) and Clerk Maxwell from the fifties onwards. As the gist of their discoveries percolated to the layman, he realized how ill his ordinary notions of his environment corresponded to the results of scientific research; he was awed by the grandeur of physical causation as everywhere his mental eye saw round him, " rank on rank, the army of unalterable law." The new ideas in physics, however, did not directly affect those on which his intellectual life was founded. It was otherwise when he learnt from geology and literary scholarship that neither the world nor the Old Testament itself was put together at the time and in the way that he believed the Bible to teach. Still more staggering were the theories of the naturalists and biologists, such as Darwin, Wallace, Huxley, and Galton, finding in evolution the key of the universe, asserting that protoplasm was the basis of all life, and explaining the origin of all diversity, from a shell-fish to Shakespeare, by accidental natural selection. It was in the sixties that the battle between orthodox theology and aggressive scientific materialism was first fairly joined, and ordinary men, who believed in Christ and yet found it difficult not to believe in science, were sadly puzzled. Even without being a Christian a man could feel, as Professor Whitehead puts it, the " radical inconsistency " between " a scientific realism, based on mechanism," and " an unwavering belief in the world of men and of the higher animals as being composed of self-determining organisms." The latter belief was fundamental not only to the dominant individualism of the day but to the whole system of law and morality on which western civilization had rested for centuries.

It was inevitable that the scientific methods which had produced such startling hypotheses as to the origin and structure of men's bodies should be applied to the study of their actions and thoughts. Morley explains the popularity of Buckle's *History of Civilization* in the late fifties by the " common readiness to extend an excited welcome to explanation whether of species or social phenomena by general laws." The economists some time before had based theories on the predictable behaviour of an economic man of their own invention. Herbert Spencer, borrowing the term " sociology " from Comte, set out in the language of science a philosophy of the evolution of the human mind and human society. His writings, among which *Social Statics*, the *Principles of Psychology*, and *The Social Organism* had appeared by the early sixties, met a popular demand and were widely read and absorbed. Laymen like Walter Bagehot began to apply scientific conceptions to politics. One result of such applications was that orthodox Liberalism, no less than orthodox Christianity, was subjected to attack. The devotee of accurate knowledge was not prejudiced in favour of parliamentary democracy and *laissez-faire*; the doctrine of the survival of the fittest might easily be misread as discouraging philanthropy; and even respect for the dignity of the individual might dissolve in the contemplation of nature " so careless of the single life."

Thus we see that forces were at work in the sixties hostile to the established order in things religious and secular. But great as was the prestige of science, crowned with its engineering and its medical laurels, it had not yet become itself the orthodox religion. Science held the position of a useful servant, and confirmed, rather than weakened, the prevailing optimism. It was a forward looking age, simple and serious, believing in the worthwhileness of things. The reigning theory still regarded the removal of restrictions as the one thing needful; it trusted human character and intellect to dominate their environment and achieve continued progress. It was an age content with its ideals, if not with its achievements, confident that it was moving on, under the guidance of Providence, to the mastery of the material world and " the creation of certain nobler races, now very dimly imagined."

CHAPTER VIII

THE NEW STATE, 1868–1900

Of Lord Palmerston's white hairs it might have been said, as it was said of Queen Elizabeth's : " When these snows melt there will be a flood." The flood came, and swept a million new voters into the electorate. Henceforward parliaments and Cabinets had to look for the approval of the working as well as of the middle classes, and working men began, though at first only in driblets, to take their places in public life. The idea that the resources of government could be used in the interests not of the great but of the lowly—an idea beyond the hopes of the Radicals of fifty years before—was now generally accepted ; and these resources had become infinitely greater. The prestige of parliament stood high as ever, and a peculiar glamour was shed over its debates by the dramatic contrast and conflict of two leaders of heroic mould, Gladstone the Oxford Churchman and Disraeli the Jewish adventurer, both men of amazing vitality, dauntless courage, and supreme oratorical power; the one excelling in moral fervour, the other in imagination and wit. Gladstone had interested the country in finance, Disraeli was to interest it in the Empire; both cared intensely for the welfare of the poor and for the honour of England abroad, though they interpreted honour in different ways. Under their alternate guidance the State came to play a larger part than ever before in the lives of their countrymen.

In the tide of democratic activity which now set in it is possible to discern distinct currents. Much was done, in the first place, in the removal of privilege—of creed, birth, and wealth. The support of the Whigs had for two centuries been drawn largely from the Protestant Dissenters, and Liberal parliaments now rapidly abolished compulsory Church rates, disestablished the Anglican Church in Ireland, and admitted Nonconformists to full membership of the ancient English universities. Privilege of social connection was abolished in the upper ranks of the Civil Service, and competitive examinations were introduced. Privilege of wealth was weakened in the army by the termination of the practice of purchasing commissions. Private patronage was abolished in the Scottish Established Kirk. The power of wealth and prestige was lessened by the introduction of voting by ballot at parliamentary elections, and the Commons gave up to the Courts their own privilege of trying election petitions.

Apart from these changes, some of the great national institutions were reformed in spite of long custom and vested interests. Cardwell gave the army for the first time an effective reserve, by reducing the term of service with the Colours, and put the supply of drafts for units overseas on a sound basis. Selborne and Cairns broke down the tiresome wall of partition between Equity and the Common Law, and established a unified system of courts administering both.

The third current expressed the intention of governments to promote positively the welfare of the poor, though at the cost of individual liberty. Much of this legislation was on lines already marked out, such as the Acts dealing with Public Health and factories and workshops, but in some cases the State assumed responsibilities of a novel order. Forster's Education Act of 1870 declared it the duty of parliament to provide opportunities for schooling for the two millions of children who were receiving none. The manifest failure of the churches to cover the ground ruled out opposition on principle, but while the government offended some bodies of opinion by sanctioning unsectarian religious teaching in the schools to be erected by public money, it disgusted Nonconformists by further encouraging denominational schools by grants from the Exchequer.

While such legislation aimed at helping the poor directly, laws were also passed to enable the poor to help themselves. The development of trade union activity in the sixties was rudely checked by a decision of the Queen's Bench in 1867 imperilling the societies' very existence. Despite the legislation of 1825 it was held that a trade union which by reason of its specified objects could be described as an association " in restraint of trade "—and very many trade unions could be so described—was not entitled to the protection of the law against defaulting officials or, it would seem, against anyone else. The Liberal government was induced in 1871 to free such unions from this vague taint of illegality and to allow them to sue defaulting officials without becoming suable themselves ; but at the same time it redefined the crime of " molesting and obstructing " in such a way as to make picketing of any kind practically impossible. Here it would make no concession, and the unionists had to wait till the Conservatives came into power after the election of 1874. An Act of the following year allowed peaceful picketing, and declared that no act by a group of workmen, if done as part of a trade dispute, should be punishable unless it would have been a criminal offence on the part of a single person.

This change in the law was the more important in that between the passings of the Liberal and Conservative measures the number of trade unionists in the country may perhaps have doubled. It is from this period that the continuous life of several of the great national societies dates. The Amalgamated Society of Railway Servants arose in 1872. The miners improved their organization and in 1874 secured the return of two of their number to parliament. About 1870 the Lancashire cotton operatives began to play their part, working like the miners for legislative protection. A Mines Regulation Act was in fact passed in 1872, and the textile workers obtained a $56\frac{1}{2}$ hour week by law soon afterwards. About the same time the engineering and building trades won their nine-hour day by strikes, enforced or threatened, and that despite the disapproval of their headquarters staff, who preferred not to risk their huge benefit funds but to work through parliament and use methods of conciliation when possible. Meanwhile the meetings of the Trade Union Congress, annual from 1871, were laying the foundations of labour solidarity and providing, in the elected Parliamentary Committee, the germ of a general staff to replace the Junta of the sixties. The

Congress of 1874 claimed to represent nearly 1,200,000 members; so formidable did trade unionism appear that a National Federation of Associated Employers of Labour was formed to counteract it. But the fortunes of the movement, like the national prosperity, were at their peak, and the strikes of the lean years that followed were as futile as those of the boom period had been successful.

The wonderful prosperity which Britain enjoyed in the third quarter of the century culminated in the early seventies. Her annual imports averaged 286 millions in the five years ending 1869, 346 millions in the five years ending 1874; the exports of British produce, 181 millions in the former period, 235 millions in the second, an increase far outweighing the rise in prices. Between 1868 and 1873 no less than nine and a half millions of taxation were remitted, yet the revenue from taxes increased by four and a half millions. Over forty-six millions of debt were paid off in the same period. In the following year the sugar duty was repealed and the income tax reduced to twopence in the pound. Moreover, wages had much more than kept pace with the rise in prices; retail prices had risen 20 per cent. over the average of 1850, but wages over 50 per cent., and there was less unemployment than at any other time in the half-century. Then the tide turned : the year 1874 started a period of falling prices and industrial and commercial depression. The money value of British exports in the following twenty-five years actually declined. In the slumps of 1879 and 1886 the percentage of unemployment rose to more than tenfold the figure of 1872, and more than 10 per cent. of the working population in the trades concerned.

The general explanation of the change is clear. England, the pioneer of the new industry, had been hitherto its monopolist. The economic development of Europe and America had meant wider markets for British goods, in particular for British iron and machinery. The acceleration of transport had brought these markets nearer. While other countries were struggling towards nationhood or adapting themselves to the new civilization, Britain had become the world's workshop, as she was already its banker and its carrier. France, her only rival, had never made up the ground lost in the great war, which paralysed her own industry and commerce while stimulating the British. The early seventies, when the world was engaged in war or post-war reconstruction, gave great opportunities to British manufacturers, and the opening of the Suez Canal in 1869 encouraged shipbuilding. But overproduction and unwise investment produced a crisis; though the crisis passed, things were never the same again; thenceforward Germany and America began to exploit their own resources behind high tariffs, and their competition became a permanent feature. For instance it appears that up to 1870 Great Britain produced half the total pig-iron output of the world; by 1903 her proportion had shrunk to a fifth, less than that of Germany and less than half that of the United States. Moreover, the progress of metallurgy had lessened her relative importance. England had risen to greatness on foundations of coal and iron, but for many purposes iron was now being superseded by steel, and the new processes in steel-making favoured foreign ores.

Nevertheless, in the iron and steel trade the set-back of the later seventies was only temporary. The same is true of the shipping trade; in spite of, or because of, such sudden shocks as the change to iron ships, and steel ships, the British mercantile marine flourished unrivalled. England remained too the chief producer of coal till the end of the century, and the proportion of her coal exported rose from an eighth of her output in 1870 to a quarter in 1900. But the case was very different as regards agriculture. To the Land the golden age ended suddenly and finally with the opening up of the new world

by railway and steamship. Trade depression
and bad harvests began the farmers' ruin; cheap
foodstuffs from abroad completed it. How
could they compete with the virgin soil of the
Mississippi valley now that ocean passages were
short and freights low? They gave up the
attempt, and turned from corn-growing to
cattle. Between 1871 and 1901 the acreage
under corn in England shrank from over eight
to under six millions, while permanent pasture
increased. But here too disaster impended.
Beef poured in during the eighties from North
and South America, mutton in the nineties from
New Zealand; cheese, butter and wool likewise.
Now, though not till now, the proportion of
imported food rose rapidly. Landlords lost
their capital and had to reduce rents. Farmers
made what use they might of improved machinery and scientific discoveries, and turned largely
to dairy-farming. Labourers' average weekly
wages rose by half-a-crown between 1871 and
1901, but fourteen shillings was a poor wage
enough, even when a man could find employment; and the new farming system needed less
hands. So hundreds of thousands migrated into
the towns or overseas, and there were a third of
a million fewer labourers on English and Welsh
farms in 1901 than thirty years before. Those
who remained were consoled by the vote in

1884, and since 1872 the possibility of collective bargaining was not wholly unknown even to them.

This gloomy picture is not true of the wage-earning classes as a whole after 1874. Unemployment was widespread in 1878–9 and again in 1884–7 and 1892–4, but on the whole employment appears to have been regular. Money wages fell a little in the seventies, but otherwise were stationary or rose slightly ; prices however fell by 40 per cent. between 1873 and 1898, while sugar and tea fell over 50 per cent. Thus real wages rose steadily from the late seventies to the end of the century, when they stood over 80 per cent. above the level of 1850. In this period wages rose more rapidly than profits, whereas between 1860 and 1874 the contrary had been the case. The consumption of corn and meat per head increased ; the consumption of tea and sugar more than doubled. Travel and correspondence were cheap ; weekly half-holidays and occasional Bank holidays were recognized ; and every child's parents were enjoined by law to have it at least taught to read and write. But of course these advantages were relative, and, even so, the generalization is a rough one. The social inquiries of the eighties and later drew anything but a complacent picture of the life of the slum-dwelling poor.

It was against this economic background that the drama of party politics in the eighties was played. The lack of confidence due to the trade depression was increased by the series of military adventures which incidentally raised the amount of the Budget from under seventy-five millions in 1874 to over a hundred millions in 1885. A blight of futility was falling on politics, in which the solidarity of the nation was riven and the prestige of parliament declined. Gladstone's name was still mighty with the electorate, to which his oratorical progresses taught politicians more and more to appeal; but he could control neither votes in the House of Commons nor events outside. In 1875 and 1876 two men entered parliament who were better attuned to the forces of the day and who were both to affect profoundly the future of the Empire. Charles Stewart Parnell, an Irish Protestant landlord, personified the intense nationalism of the century; Joseph Chamberlain, the Radical mayor of Birmingham, its spirit of constructive democracy at home and constructive imperialism overseas. For the moment it was in parliamentary politics that their personalities were to tell. Chamberlain represented the element in the Liberal party hostile to things established, such as the Church and his Whig colleagues; he had the backing of the new national organization of the party, founded to extend throughout the country the methods of democratic efficiency introduced ten years before by the Birmingham Caucus. Parnell, supported by a band of obedient henchmen, represented the majority of the Irish people. Ireland had at last come to her own—at least as regards attention—and Parnell was the man of the hour.

To British statesmen the Irish question was primarily one of repressing crime and maintaining order. For this purpose one government after another felt compelled to ask parliament for more drastic powers than the ordinary law allowed. But it could not be maintained that Irish crime sprang merely from original sin ; it was the result of an unhealthy social situation. Apart from the fundamental misfortune that English politicians did not understand Irish minds, there were three elements in the Irish question as Pitt left it : the economic, the religious, and the purely political. Had the first found timely settlement, it is possible that the others would have given comparatively little trouble. But the abuses of an indefensible system of land tenure continued unchecked until the famine of 1846–7 brought catastrophe ; thousands died, and the survivors, on both sides of the Atlantic, cherished an implacable hatred of English government. Even after the famine no constructive measures were taken for twenty years, and yet free corn for England meant ruin to Irish farmers. At length in 1870 Gladstone carried the first Irish Land Act, compelling the landlord to allow his tenant compensation for any improvement the tenant had made, and forbidding eviction except for failure to pay rent. But the Irish peasant lived so near starvation that any untoward circumstance, such as the bad harvests of the seventies, reduced him to penury. Frequent evictions and general distress led in 1879 to the foundation of the Land League, aimed primarily against the exaction of unfair rent. After the House of Lords had rejected a bill passed by the Commons for compensating tenants unreasonably evicted, there followed a sorry warfare between Irish government and people, waged on the one side by boycotting, intimidation, cattle-maiming, and agrarian murder, on the other by coercive legislation and arrests; within its own walls the House of Commons countered the Parnellites' new weapon of parliamentary obstruction with the newer weapon of the closure. Another Land Act was passed in 1881 further stabilizing the peasant's position; his rent was to be fixed by a Land Court for a fifteen-year term, and he was to be encouraged to buy his holding by an advance of money from the State. But this did not bring conciliation, and when in the following year events began at last to move in that direction, the hopes of peace perished along with the victims of the Phœnix Park murderers, struck down by the enemies of England, Parnell, and the Land League alike.

The two other elements in the situation, religion and politics, had been inextricable so long as Roman Catholics as such were refused political rights. The Relief Act of 1829 left over two separate points of attack — the Established Church and the Union. As early as 1815 Peel, then Chief Secretary, had become convinced that the Irish Catholics would be satisfied with no arrangement which should " continue to maintain a separate Church Establishment for the religion of one-fifth of the population." But again no bold step was taken till Gladstone became Prime Minister. After Irish Disestablishment in 1869, the religious factors which most embarrassed British governments were the impalpable but unavoidable truths that religious passions divided Irishmen of the south and north and that Irish Catholic priests were the political mentors of their flocks.

Thus the great religious obstacle to friendship between the two islands had been removed by the eighties; the agrarian problem, though

acute, had been tackled, and a development of
Land Acts might suggest the lines of a solution.
Lord Spencer's viceroyalty (1882–5) showed that
mere crime could be suppressed. The political
issue remained. The Union had never had the
consent of the Irish people, and Daniel O'Connell
had led an agitation for its repeal. That movement had collapsed in the forties; the Fenian
agitation for an Irish Republic in the sixties was
a much less serious affair. But after 1880 there
were sixty-one Irish Home Rulers in the House
of Commons, and more than half of them followed
Parnell—a man who valued neither the welfare
of England nor her respect as anything beside
the fulfilment of the desires of Irish nationalism.
Peel had in 1815 expressed his belief that " an
honest despotic Government would be by far
the fittest Government for Ireland," and many
Chief Secretaries have probably thought so since.
But the play of parties and the growth of democracy in Great Britain made any permanent
system of coercion impossible, while the rise of a
compact and intransigent Home Rule party at
Westminster suggested that unsatisfied Irishmen
might make government difficult even in England.

The proposal to repeal the Act of Union had
never been taken seriously in Great Britain.
But in 1885 federalism was in the air, and the

apparent impossibility of governing Ireland from London except by repeated coercion laws induced statesmen of both British parties to toy with the idea of giving her some measure of self-government.   Neither party had decided on a policy when Parnell, hoping better things from the Conservatives, swung the Irish vote, first in parliament and later at the polls, against the Liberals. The general election of 1885, the first held under the new Reform Act, gave the result which Gladstone had deprecated—a Liberal majority dependent on the votes of the Parnellites.   Believing a prompt settlement of the Irish question to be nevertheless of vital importance, Gladstone convinced himself that the time was ripe to set up a subordinate parliament in Dublin with an executive responsible to it.   The leader of neither section of his divided party, neither Hartington the Whig, nor Chamberlain the Radical, was prepared to follow him ; nor, it soon appeared, was the House of Commons, nor yet the electorate.   So after the general election of 1886, which followed the defeat of Gladstone's first Home Rule bill, Lord Salisbury took office, prepared to pacify Ireland by twenty years of resolute government.

Salisbury had the support of 316 Conservatives and 74 Liberal Unionists, for Gladstone's insistence on prematurely forcing the Home

Rule issue had irreparably shattered the Liberal party. Despite the suddenness of his decision, Gladstone carried the bulk of his followers with him, which Peel in 1846 failed to do ; but whereas Peel passed his corn bill into law, Gladstone never put Home Rule on the statute-book, neither in 1886 nor yet in 1893, when after Parnell's death Irish votes helped to carry the second Home Rule bill through the Commons against the majority of members from Great Britain. By then the question was one no longer of mere administrative expediency but of fundamental principle. Home Rule was resisted in Ulster with a passionate intensity rooted in racial and religious antagonism. Many in England and Scotland shared this emotion ; many were disgusted by the callous disregard shown by the Irish members for British tradition and Irish lives, and many believed that Gladstone had spoken sober truth in earlier days when he described Parnell and his party as "marching through rapine to the dismemberment of the Empire." The action of the Lords in rejecting the second Home Rule bill aroused no resentment in the country, and the general election of 1895 inaugurated ten years of Unionist government. All this time and longer the demand for Irish Home Rule lay buried and out of mind, but buried like Pindar's giant under

Etna, ready to pour out again its fiery torrent at the appointed hour.

In 1894 Gladstone retired from politics. He was 84, and it was sixty years since his first acceptance of office. Ever since 1886 it had been the Irish question alone which had kept him in harness. To him it was the supreme issue. But other men cared for other things : for the further democratization of government, central and local, and for using the State's power constructively to promote the welfare of the weak.

On the side of political democracy the fifteen years after 1880 were marked by the extension of the franchise to some million and three-quarters of new voters, including householders in country districts ; by the dethronement of the Justices of the Peace from the government of the countryside, which had been theirs for at least three centuries, and by the establishment of elected councils in county, district, and parish, and even in Greater London. As the councils proved their competence, new functions were granted them, and they gradually absorbed the *ad hoc* bodies which earlier parliaments, suspicious of the local authorities they knew, had scattered over the country. In 1902 the new tendency culminated in the transfer to the councils of the powers of the elected School Boards, and only the Poor Law remained under separate administration. Moreover in national politics attempts were made to democratize the selection of their candidates and programmes by the great parties—a field in which the Birmingham Caucus was pioneer—and the Primrose League was founded to popularize Conservatism.

The Primrose League exploited the indirect political influence of women. Women had already been admitted to the municipal franchise, and made eligible for School Boards, and in 1886 a bill giving them the parliamentary vote passed its second reading in the Commons. Even the law of property was reformed in their favour. In 1882 all married women were given by statute that control over their own property which had hitherto been available only to the daughters of the rich. Women factory inspectors, two in number, were appointed for the first time in 1892.

Gladstone complained in 1885 of " the leaning of both parties to socialism." The new radicalism of Chamberlain and Sir Charles Dilke on his own side was rivalled by the " Tory democracy " of Lord Randolph Churchill. As early as 1867 a Conservative Minister had not shrunk from picturing the State as " the parent of the country " in speaking on a factory bill, and factory legislation had been the thin end of the collectivistic wedge. The wedge was now hammered further in. The principle of a statutory day was extended to shops ; factory acts became more detailed, and provisions for health and safety were applied to places where only men worked, to domestic workshops in the case of dangerous trades, and eventually to outworkers' homes. The curious doctrine of the Courts that an employer was not liable to his employee for damage caused by a fellow-workman was modified in 1880, and nullified in 1897 by legislation compelling masters to insure their workmen against the risks of their employment. Further interference with freedom of contract resulted from the great railway company amalgamations ; in 1893 maximum rates were fixed for goods traffic, and powers were given to the Board of Trade to limit the hours of *men's* labour—a most important precedent.

The series of statutes encouraging local authorities, in town and country, to provide houses or plots of land for working men represents two forms of socialistic action : the compulsory demolition or acquisition of private property, and the supply of services by the State. In the former Irish necessities gave a lead to Great Britain ; examples of the latter appear in the Acts allowing towns to construct, own, and operate gas and electrical works and tramways, to erect libraries and baths, and to distribute milk. School instruction for children, for which the State took direct responsibility in 1870, was within ten years made compulsory and universal, and in 1891 supplied free, at the cost of two millions a year. This was socialism full-blown, though enacted by Conservatives and Liberal Unionists, and quite as radical in its way as Sir William Harcourt's 1894 Budget which raised the limit of exemption from income tax and introduced a graduated succession duty rising to 8 per cent. on the largest estates.

All these measures were passed by parliamentary majorities that would have blushed to be called socialist. Their legislative methods were typically English—fragmentary, gradual, illogical, based on plain experience and concrete instances, not deduced from theory. The reports of Royal Commissions on Housing and Sweating and the researches of Charles Booth and his assistants unearthed facts which could not be ignored. At the same time the example of Bismarck's new industrial policy in Germany showed how effective the positive action of the State might prove. The part of theory was subsidiary, to sap the resistance of the rigid *laissez-faire* thought and create a favourable mental atmosphere. Unconsciously Members found it possible to think of society, or the community, protecting its own standards of life, not merely of the rich being taxed or restricted for the benefit of the poor. After all, socialism and individualism are matters of degree, and the same proposal can often be advocated from both points of view.

But if socialist theory played a negligible part at Westminster, it was beginning to permeate certain sections of the intellectual middle class and, through them, the masses of organized labour. Practically non-existent in 1880, by 1900 it had progressed remarkably. Able men to whom the Liberalism of the early eighties made little appeal found inspiration in the criticisms launched at capitalism by Mill among the dead, and Karl Marx and Henry George among the living—criticisms developed in the one case out of Utilitarian orthodoxy, in the other based on the native English socialism of the twenties. It was now possible to regard the industrial revolution with something like detachment; artists like William Morris and Bernard Shaw found it as repellent as did the economic historians, and they both laid the blame for its ugliness and vulgarity, its cruelty and waste, at the door of excessive individualism. Societies were founded to urge the substitution of public for private ownership and control of wealth; while some believed with Marx in the catastrophic dispossession of the capitalist, the Fabians, with

Shaw and Sidney Webb at their head, devoted themselves to teaching the new democracy how to introduce socialism by legislative instalments. It was not till late in the eighties that these ideas made any impression on the working classes. The terrible depression which followed the boom of 1874 hit the trade unions and their members hard. The movement weathered the storm, but with diminished vitality, and to the unemployed who tramped the streets in 1884–7 trade unionism seemed as useless as Free Trade or the Liberalism which their own leaders professed. Opinion was thus prepared for the lure of the " New Unionism," inspired by socialist ideals and apparently vindicated by the conspicuous success of the London dockers' strike of 1889. Skilfully organized by John Burns, Tom Mann, and Ben Tillett, three leaders of the new militant socialist type, the strikers won much sympathy outside, and their victory resulted not only in an extension of unionism to the ranks of unskilled labour but in a general renewal of interest in the movement. By 1892 membership totalled about a million and a half, or 20 per cent. of the adult male manual wage-earners. It was a triumph for socialism ; in 1890 the Trade Union Congress, hitherto suspicious of politics, declared for a general Eight Hours bill and for extended State and municipal action ; three years later many trade unionists joined the Independent Labour Party, founded with a socialist programme by Keir Hardie to wean the working class from Liberalism.   Hitherto Gladstone and Bright had been their heroes, and it was not till after Gladstone's death in 1898 that definite steps were taken to create a working class parliamentary party independent of Liberals and Conservatives.   In 1900 the Labour Representation Committee, afterwards known as the Labour Party, came into existence with official trade union backing and with Mr. Ramsay Macdonald as its first secretary.

It is natural to wonder whether the Liberal party would have been spared this loss of its left wing if Gladstone had persisted in his intention not to take office in 1880.   It is true that he drew the almost idolatrous loyalty of thousands of working men ; on the other hand, it was his precipitate action in the Irish question— " an old man in a hurry " he was called—which drove Chamberlain out of the party ; and Chamberlain was the Liberal statesman whose views made the strongest appeal to labour.   Had some Whig magnate become Prime Minister in 1880, could Chamberlain nevertheless have built up a radical-collectivist party capable of uniting the allegiance of wage-earners and middle class Liberals ?

M

CHAPTER IX

WHEN the sixties ended Britain no longer enjoyed the predominant place among the Powers which had been hers half a century before. The Vienna settlement had been broken up by forces over which she had no control. Her influence had counted in the making of Italy, but hardly in the making of Germany. All she could do, when war broke out between France and Prussia, was to negotiate with each belligerent a treaty for the defence of Belgium against the other; and, when Russia announced that in defiance of treaty provisions she intended to keep warships in the Black Sea, to insist on the need of European sanction. If it was an advantage for her, as Gladstone declared, to "keep entire in her own hands the means of estimating her own obligations upon the various states of facts as they arise," she had also the disadvantages of remaining isolated in Europe for a generation.

But British interests were less than ever confined to Europe. Disraeli spoke in 1872 of the duty of " reconstructing as much as possible our Colonial Empire," and alike on military and economic grounds this vast reservoir of man-power and raw materials was claiming closer attention. Annexation projects previously discouraged were carried through by the Conservative government in the Pacific, South Africa, and on the Indian frontier. It was the East which most fascinated and inspired Disraeli's exotic genius. He pictured his country as " the most powerful of Oriental States," and as " really more an Asiatic power than a European." He it was who passed through a reluctant parliament the bill to make the Queen Empress of India, and he it was who, realizing the importance of the Suez Canal (opened in 1869) to British communications with the East, purchased for £4,000,000 the shares in the Canal Company owned by the Khedive of Egypt.

Both in Central Asia and in the Near East the Power which seemed most antagonistic to England was Russia. Her successive advances to Samarcand and Khiva, with the threat to Merv and Herat, and her opening of relations with Afghanistan caused much nervousness as to her intentions in the minds of British statesmen ; the results were a reversal of Indian frontier policy and the outbreak of the second Afghan war. In the Levant her desires to dominate the eastern Balkans and extend her frontiers in Armenia were held to menace British communications with the East. " Constantinople," said Disraeli, " is the key of India."

Just before he came into power in 1874 Disraeli had blamed the Liberals for showing too much energy in domestic legislation and not enough in foreign affairs ; next year the re-opening of the Eastern question gave him a golden opportunity to reassert the prestige of England in the councils of Europe. Turkey's failure to improve her administration in the interval following the Crimean war made insurrections on the part of her Christian subjects inevitable. In 1875 various outbreaks occurred and intervention by the Powers impended. Disraeli refused to allow the three eastern monarchies to keep the initiative in their own hands, and, believing that the disintegration of the Sultan's dominions must lead to war and confusion, he revived the Palmerstonian policy of championing Turkey. Encouraged by British support the Turks showed their usual intransigence, and in April 1877 Russia declared war on them. Despite assurances that Russia would not touch Constantinople, the Persian Gulf, Egypt, or the Suez Canal Disraeli felt no security, and for many months tension was extreme. In the spring of 1878, when Russia demurred to submitting the treaty she had by then imposed on Turkey to the free judgment of the Powers, the Cabinet decided to call out the reserve, to bring troops from India, and if necessary to occupy Cyprus and Alexandretta; the fleet was ordered to Constantinople. Russia eventually gave way, and the Congress of Berlin, at which Disraeli (now Lord Beaconsfield) and Lord Salisbury represented England, toned down those articles of the treaty which maintained Russian predominance in European Turkey; in view, however, of Russia's acquisitions in Armenia and the danger that she might thence threaten either the Persian Gulf or the Suez Canal, Beaconsfield gave Turkey a guarantee of her Asiatic dominions and in return received Cyprus from the Porte to enable England to fulfil the obligation.

The Government's reluctance at an earlier stage to allow the Sultan to be coerced was vehemently condemned by the Liberal Opposition. The barbarity with which the Turks had suppressed a Bulgarian outbreak in 1876 had incited Gladstone to pour out the vials of his indignation in a notable pamphlet, and aroused in the country an almost unprecedented interest in foreign affairs. When later the " Jingo " hostility to Russia was ranged on the opposite side, the division of feeling cut deep, and it did much to embitter party spirit in the eighties.

Having acquired Cyprus England was now to establish herself in Egypt. Her coming was the result of no deep-laid plans, but of Egyptian incompetence and French shortsightedness. The extravagance and insolvency of the Khedive Ismail led in 1876 to unofficial intervention by France and England on behalf of their nationals, then to Dual Control in financial matters; financial involved political responsibility, and when in 1882 native grievances resulted in riot and revolution, England intervened by sea and land to check them, France refusing to co-operate. This was the beginning of the occupation of Egypt by Britain alone—an occupation never intended to be permanent, but continually prolonged by the absence of any alternative form of stable government. For twenty years it was a thorn in the side of the French, who lost no opportunity of making British administration difficult.

Responsibilities in Egypt created responsibilities further south, in the Sudan, where Egyptian troops under British officers had for many years been warring against the fierce slave-trading tribes. In 1881 the fanatical Mahdi stirred up a successful revolt and two years later he cut to pieces an Egyptian force under Hicks

Pasha, its English commander. In fulfilment of the policy of abandoning the Sudan, adopted by the Khedive on British advice, the Gladstone Cabinet in January 1884 took the fatal step of sending out for its accomplishment the erratic military genius, Charles Gordon. Owing partly to unclear instructions, partly to his own temperament, Gordon was cut off at Khartum, and a relief expedition despatched to save him arrived too late.

The wave of indignation which swept the country at the news of Gordon's death revived a sense of the Liberals' incapacity to protect British interests abroad, which their management of South African affairs had aroused some years earlier. Here a legacy of trouble had been inherited from the Conservatives. Ever since the Dutch farmers had trekked north from Cape Colony in 1836 to avoid British officials and British missionaries, their political status had been rather indefinite, and the different attitudes of British and Boers to the natives caused constant friction. First into Natal, and then north of the Orange River, British rule pursued the emigrants. But British rule was almost as lacking in continuity as British policy. In 1854 it was withdrawn from the Orange River territory, leaving independent Boer communities south as well as north of the Vaal, and Sir George

Grey's project, in 1857, for a federal union came
to nothing. When similar projects were mooted
fifteen years later, disputes with both Boer
republics had soured relations, and there was no
response to the initiative taken by Lord Carnarvon, the Conservative Colonial Secretary. Influenced by the breakdown of government in the
Transvaal and by the menace of the Zulu military power, Carnarvon in 1877 high-handedly
annexed the republic to the British Empire
without due consultation of the inhabitants.
The grant of popular government, which might
have alleviated the grievance, was postponed,
and at the end of 1880 the Transvaal Boers rose
in arms and invaded Natal. Overtures of peace
were already in train when the British force was
defeated at Majuba Hill. The Liberal government decided to continue the negotiations, and
a Convention was signed with the Boers whereby
the act of annexation was revoked, Great Britain
retaining " suzerainty " and control of the
Transvaal's foreign relations. The Liberals were
hotly censured at home for making this concession
without taking military steps to wipe out the
memory of the Boer victory at Majuba.

By this time the idea of the Empire was grip-
ping the public imagination, and people at home
were coming to understand its dual character as
at once an alliance of self-governing communities

and a constellation of subject dependencies ruled from London. The first aspect was emphasized by the publication of books like Seeley's *Expansion of England*, by the foundation of the Imperial Federation League in 1884, and by the meeting of the first Colonial Conference three years later. The importance of the second was multiplied by the construction of ocean cables and continental railways. Thanks to machinery, production and transport could be speeded up and colonial enterprise made commercially profitable.

Official reluctance to incur increased commitments overseas was shaken by the enterprise shown by other Powers in securing colonies, with the probability that they would adopt exclusive tariffs ; by French acquisitions in Tunis, West Africa and Indo-China, and by the staking out of German claims in 1883–5 in the Pacific and in Central and South-West Africa. There was a general fear of being too late in the race, and in the next fifteen years an immense amount of tropical and subtropical territory was annexed by England alone. British New Guinea, North Borneo, and Upper Burma were all added to the Empire in the eighties, and in Africa the way to annexation was prepared by the pioneer activities of great Chartered Companies with rights of trade and administration in the Niger region, in

East Africa, and in the interior of South Africa. Here the vision and daemonic energy of Cecil Rhodes were working for the creation of a united dominion stretching from the southern ocean to the confines of the Great Lakes, to be developed by British and Dutch together under the protection of the Crown. Owing largely to his initiative, the region west of the Transvaal became British in 1885, and the vast territories to the north, now known by his name, on both sides of the Zambesi, were colonized.

At the same time the discovery of reef gold on the Witwatersrand promised to transform the patriarchal life of the Transvaal farmers through an infusion of hustling adventurers. Between two such discordant and not very tactful elements there was great danger of friction, and within ten years the refusal of the Transvaal government to treat these " Outlanders " as citizens provoked a crisis. The outbreak, and the failure, of a rising planned by some of the British population with Rhodes' connivance confirmed the Boers in their intransigence and in their contempt for British military capacity. The British government asserted suzerain rights which the Transvaal authorities denied, and in 1899 war broke out. The end came in 1902 with the re-annexation of the Transvaal and the Orange Free State to the British Empire, but initial defeats and hopes of victory deferred did much to destroy such complacency as the pageantry of the Queen's Diamond Jubilee had fostered a few years before.

The new interest in the Empire was not only manifested in additions to its area. Chamberlain chose the Colonial Office in 1895 with intent to exalt colonial policy as Disraeli had exalted foreign policy twenty years earlier. In his eight years of office he contrived to convince administrators overseas of a new spirit of sympathy and co-operation in Downing Street, and he did more than any of his predecessors to promote the sentiment of unity. A penny post throughout the Empire was introduced and ocean cables were subsidized. Colonial government stocks were ranked as British trustee securities and loans for railways and harbours to open up the "undeveloped estates" of the Empire were advanced to Crown Colonies. The Board of Trade set up a branch to disseminate commercial information, an imperial Department of Agriculture was established in the West Indies to promote research, and schools of tropical medicine studied the causes of malaria. By the end of the century British emigrants were settling more and more within the Empire, rather than in the United States ; colonial governments had begun to give preferences to British imports, and in the

South African war they sent voluntary contingents to fight on the British side. Thought had moved far from the days, a generation before, when the permanent head of the Colonial Office could speak of Canada as " a colony which is no good to us and has no real care for us." But Chamberlain was not satisfied. In 1903 he urged the colonial governments to take a larger share in imperial defence, and at home he divided the country and his party on the issue whether the United Kingdom should return the preferences granted by the colonies to the extent of taxing food imported from foreign countries.

Less material forces worked to the same end. During much of the lifetime of the Prince Consort and for many years after his death the Court had been none too popular; but as the century waned Victoria became an institution beloved as well as revered by the people whose sentiments she shared, and a sunset splendour warmed the last decades of her long reign. This personal affection helped in creating for the Crown a new importance as a magnet of common loyalty from communities living all over the world in every stage of social and political development. Africans and Asiatics to whom the Common Law, parliament, and the British islands themselves meant nothing could unite in venerating the Great White Queen; and the knowledge of this truth reacted on her subjects at home. Nor was it an accident that the two first meetings of Colonial Premiers in London were held on the occasions of the Queen's two Jubilees; imperial co-operation became thereby associated with the person of the Sovereign. The dual sentiment was strengthened by the writings of Rudyard Kipling; directly in his poems, more subtly in his prose stories, he popularized the idea of a common imperial patriotism transcending an infinite diversity of birth and circumstance and ennobled by a common ideal of service.

The new imperialism did not increase the love of foreign nations for England, and in the last twenty years of the century there was no single friend on whom she could rely. Fear of Russian intentions in Persia, Central Asia and the Far East was chronic, so much so that to many another Anglo-Russian war appeared inevitable. Relations with France too were almost consistently bad. As soon as she recovered from the collapse of 1870 France devoted her energies to rebuilding a colonial empire, and she seemed to lose no opportunity of thwarting British aims and hampering British trade in Africa and Indo-China; but in 1887 she missed what was perhaps her last chance of negotiating the British out of Egypt, and eleven years later the Anglo-

Egyptian reconquest of the Sudan gave the deathblow to French pretensions to a footing in the Nile valley. Thus France and Russia were the Powers which England regarded as her natural enemies, and it was against them that the secret agreements of 1887 were directed, by which she undertook to co-operate with Italy and Austria-Hungary in preserving the *status quo* in the Mediterranean and the Balkans.

With Germany it was otherwise. Here there was no tradition of hostility, and so long as Bismarck was in power relations were usually friendly. Convinced that what Germany now needed was peace, Bismarck worked for two objects : to prevent France from securing an ally whose support might encourage her to take up arms for the recovery of Alsace-Lorraine, and to establish such an influence over both Austria-Hungary and Russia as to deter them from pursuing their Balkan rivalries to the point of war. His policy was therefore to keep on good terms with both empires, while recognizing that in the last resort Germany could not allow Austria to be crushed by Russia. But if Russia could be checked without Germany being involved in war, so much the better. Consequently, when the Balkan situation became threatening in the later eighties, Bismarck encouraged the Mediterranean agreement pledging Italy and England to join with Austria in resisting Russian aggression. He even played with the idea of an Anglo-German alliance, despite the recent colonial controversies, and made definite overtures to this end to Lord Salisbury. They were not accepted, but treaties were signed between the two countries in 1890 providing amicably for the apportionment of territories in East Africa and for the cession of Heligoland to Germany.

After Bismarck's fall in 1890 smaller men found the game as he had played it too difficult. Russia was allowed to drift away into closer and closer connection with France, while the new emphasis laid on colonial aspirations, which with Bismarck were never more than secondary, increased the chances of conflict with England. Thanks largely to the emotional and melodramatic temperament of the young Emperor William, German policy in these years lacked consistency and proportion, and was expressed with a brusqueness most irritating to other nations. Holding always to the Austrian alliance as fundamental, the Emperor and his advisers zigzagged between the desire for cooperation with England and the lure of a continental league, including Russia, directed against England. Nor had they any coherent colonial policy; their object was apparently to exploit every difficulty in which another State might find itself to exact "compensations" for Germany in some part of the world.

As Africa was the prey of imperialistic appetites and international rivalry in the eighties, so was China in the nineties. England, under Palmerston's leadership, had borne the brunt in the forcible opening of China to European trade, and the principal share in this trade, particularly in the Yangtse valley, had long been hers. Meanwhile Russia, sweeping across Asia ever eastward to the Pacific coast, had assumed political interests in Manchuria and Korea. Fearing Russian aggression on the mainland, the British in 1885 seized Port Hamilton in the Korean archipelago ; but this occupation lasted only for two years, and it was not till after China's crushing defeat by the Japanese in the war of 1894-5 that the scramble for her territory began. First Japan abortively, then with greater success Germany, Russia, Britain, and France planted themselves at strategic points on Chinese soil. Britain, it is true, admitted the principle of equal economic opportunity for all nations and in 1900 concluded a treaty on this basis with Germany ; it included a renunciation by both Powers of further "territorial advantages" for themselves. But by this time foreign aggression had aroused among the Chinese a storm of indignation which expressed itself violently in the

Boxer outbreak. When the Powers united to protect and avenge their nationals, Russia took the opportunity of occupying Manchuria and building a railway southward through the Liao-tung peninsula. This advance, threatening both Korea and Peking, was an obvious challenge to the Japanese, but it alarmed England also ; as early as 1895 she had refused to join the other European Powers in compelling Japan to restore the spoils of victory to China, and now in 1902, in order to keep the ring clear for Japan's impending struggle with Russia, the two island empires entered into a defensive alliance.

For England the Japanese alliance was a remarkable departure from tradition. But the events of the last few years—the clash with France in the Sudan and the hostile attitude of foreign countries during the Boer war—had brought home to her the dangers of isolation, and indeed before this, in 1898, she had made overtures to both Russia and Germany. The first were abruptly cut short by events in China. With regard to Germany the initiative was Chamberlain's. Believing that, whereas England had important differences with Russia and France in Asia and Africa, no real conflict of interests sundered the two kindred nations facing one another across the North Sea, in the spring of 1898 Chamberlain obtained authority to suggest an alliance to Germany ; negotiations were continued in 1899, but broke down owing to the German statesmen's fear of compromising themselves with Russia, with whom they were then on friendly terms, should England play them false, and also to their hope that England might be induced to offer more favourable terms later on.   The question was reopened in 1901, when Edward VII had succeeded to the throne and Lord Lansdowne to the Foreign Office.   The implications of an alliance were seriously considered in London, and also in Berlin, where the principle was approved.   But the possibility of a British accord with France and Russia, and the consequent fatefulness of the present decision, were not sufficiently realized.   Believing that she could afford to wait, Germany made it a condition that Britain should undertake obligations towards Austria-Hungary and Italy as well as herself, and this put an end to the negotiations.   Popular feeling in the two countries was undoubtedly not propitious to an alliance, and it would have been difficult for a British parliament to accept the definite commitments on which the Germans insisted.   But the results of the failure were momentous.   As they had warned Berlin, the British government now turned to the opposite camp, and in 1904 came to a full political understanding with France.

These years were also important in the story of Anglo-American relations. It is of good augury for a world in which the influence of the English-speaking communities is increasing that since 1783 so many important differences between the United States and the British Empire have been settled by peaceful means. Thus the Maine boundary was fixed in 1842, and the Oregon boundary in 1846 : but neither of these settlements set half so valuable a precedent as did the arbitration of 1871–2 on the *Alabama* claims.[1] In that case a highly complicated dispute, in which " national honour " was involved on both sides, was after great difficulties submitted to a tribunal with a majority of neutral judges, and damages of over three million pounds, though regarded as grossly excessive by public opinion, were duly paid over by the British Treasury. Other American issues were referred to arbitration in the nineties, in one case—that of the Venezuelan boundary—not without heart-burnings. But neither President Cleveland's threats on that occasion, nor the rejection by the Senate of a general arbitration treaty in 1897, could prevent British opinion from siding with the United States in their war with Spain. Chamberlain spoke publicly of an alliance, and henceforward government and

[1] See p. 131.

people were alike resolved to remain on friendly terms with the great English-speaking nation now first entering on the field of world politics.

In 1899 the first International Peace Conference was held, on the Tsar's invitation, at The Hague. In his main purpose, the limitation of armaments, he failed completely, and England declined to discuss the question of the capture of enemy private property at sea in wartime. But the British delegates played a leading part in the attempt, partially successful, to establish a permanent court of international arbitration.

British foreign policy had emerged in the last fifteen years of the century from the welter of party strife. As Salisbury came to abandon that championship of a decadent Turkey which stirred the anger of Liberals, so Rosebery upheld British prestige with a vigour that Unionists could admire. Not till events in the Transvaal moved again to a crisis was feeling acutely divided, and then the division was not between parties but within the Liberal ranks. On the major issues of world politics Salisbury's calm, cautious, and conciliatory statesmanship had created a unity of opinion which served England well in the difficult and dangerous times that followed.

CHAPTER X

THE ARMED PEACE

QUEEN VICTORIA's death marked the close of an epoch in home and foreign affairs alike, as the rise of a Labour party and the search for alliances bore witness. It was no less the end of an epoch in thought and feeling. A positive age, earnest and confident, was shading off into one of doubts and difficulties, not less serious but critical and ironical. Tennyson, George Eliot, and even Browning passed into eclipse, and such masters of realism and irony as Thomas Hardy, Samuel Butler, Bernard Shaw, A. E. Housman, and J. M. Synge caught the popular ear. In the minds of larger and larger numbers of educated people, belief in the assumptions of natural science was supplanting Christianity as orthodoxy. Church-going was no longer a universal custom, and the persecution of the atheist Bradlaugh, which wasted days of parliamentary time in the eighties, would have been inconceivable in the parliament of 1906. Even in the eighties, it appeared to the lady who was to become Mrs.

Sidney Webb, the mainspring of philanthropy was no longer the service of God but the service of man.

On the material side, the progress of machinery and other inventions, the opening up of distant lands, and the development of cheap and swift transport, had made possible an unimagined standard of comfort for all but the poorest, and of luxury for the rich. Tea, coffee, and sugar were becoming cheaper. For a penny one could travel a mile by train, buy a morning and an evening newspaper, or send a letter to Australia. Electric light, telephones, and motor-cars were coming into common use. Wealth was still rapidly increasing. In the last third of the nineteenth century the sum of taxable incomes and the amount spent in wages had both doubled, and though the population of Great Britain now totalled 37 instead of 25 millions, the average of real wages had risen by over two-thirds.

But against this rosy picture must be set the damning facts brought to light by social investigators : three-tenths of the population of London were living in poverty so abject as barely to afford subsistence. For thirty years now private charity had been organized on a scale and with a skill unknown in the world's history, yet its results seemed a drop in the ocean. Where the appeal to compassion had failed, social reformers of the new type chose to appeal to the sense of injustice. It was seen at the same time how large a proportion of the workers employed in manufacture failed to secure from either factory acts or trade unions protection against overwork and underpayment. And further, though the standard of living of labour as a whole was relatively favourable in 1900, the following years showed a decline, and what a man resents is the loss of what he has become accustomed to. In this period prices were rising. Money wages, on the other hand, rose little if at all, except in certain industries such as coal and cotton, with the result that real wages were actually falling. Unemployment was not so widespread as in 1879 and the mid-eighties, but it was considerable in 1903–5, and worse in 1908–9. Revolutions, we are told, are most likely when the downtrodden are well enough off to think how much better off they might be. So it was in England in the reign of Edward VII, a foreigner might well have supposed. Better wages and education had enabled labour to organize, and brought within its horizon, as Mr. Layton puts it, the possibility of a more comfortable and dignified existence. Moreover the increase in the size of industrial establishments had in many instances put an end to the old personal relations between masters and men.

But revolutions in England are written with a small letter.

After peace had been signed with the Boers in May 1902 it was natural that the interest so long directed to South Africa should flow back in strong reaction to the condition of the people at home. Not only did the conscience and imagination of statesmen point there, but the working class had now sufficient political and industrial strength to insist that its grievances should be considered. It is typical of the shift of thought that the policy of tariff reform, which Chamberlain proposed in 1903 in the interests of imperial consolidation, should have been gradually transformed into a scheme for the protection of British manufactures. For more than twenty years a small group of " Fair Traders " had cried in the wilderness for a relaxation of Cobdenist orthodoxy under the new economic conditions, but Free Trade seemed as firmly embedded in British political thought as Magna Carta till the great ex-Radical from Birmingham thundered at the gate. Declaring that, as the result of the competition of goods produced behind German and American tariff walls, the chief British industries were doomed, if not dying, he demanded, along with taxes on imported food giving a preference to the colonies, an average 10 per cent. scientific tariff on foreign manufactured

goods. Thus protected, the wilting industries
would revive and allow a rise in the working
man's standard of living.

The bulk of the Unionist party accepted the
scheme, and laid it before the country at the
general election of 1906. What part it played
in their downfall cannot be told: they had
against them the " swing of the pendulum," the
grievances of Nonconformists and trade unionists, distrust of the new imperialism, and South
African misrepresentations as gross as those
which had helped them to victory in 1900. The
Liberals were returned to power with a huge
majority independent of Irish Nationalists and
the new group of Labour members. In the
Cabinet there sat side by side Liberal Imperialists of the Rosebery School, John Burns, the
hero of the 1889 dock strike, and the " Little
Englander " followers of Sir Henry Campbell-
Bannerman, the new Prime Minister. The party
had been out of office, with a short interval, for
twenty years, and there were long arrears of
legislation to make up. They began with the
demands of the great interests which had voted
for them, and first of the trade unions.

The subtle question, how far, and by what
right, a group of individuals can have a personality and a purpose of its own, overlaps the frontiers
of several sciences. When property or material

injury is concerned it becomes a matter for the Courts, and in these years British judges had difficult decisions to make. They had to decide, in the case of the Scottish Free Kirk, whether the continuity of a church rests in its original tenets or in the opinions of its members. They were constantly called on to evolve a theory of corporations in the case of joint-stock companies, and the growing prevalence of this method of doing business, along with the rise of great trusts and combines controlling enormous resources of capital, gave the matter an increasing importance. Similar questions, again, were involved in the development of trade unionism, and in 1901 the Taff Vale judgment awoke a storm of controversy.

A Welsh railway strike raised the issue of the liability of a trade union to pay damages for wrongful—not criminal—acts committed by its agents. It must be remembered that a large part of most trade unions' funds went to provide unemployment and other benefits, and also that trade unions occupied a unique legal position, not being technically corporations. The decision turned on the exact nature of this status. Hitherto it had been supposed that a trade union, being an unincorporated society, could not be sued in tort (a civil wrong, other than a breach of contract), but legal procedure had been developing so as to make such suits possible. In applying the new doctrine to the Amalgamated Society of Railway Servants the judges dealt a severe blow to trade union activity : any wrongful act committed by an official in the course of a trade dispute—and the legal definition of wrongful acts was large and ill-defined—might compel the union to pay thousands of pounds in damages. The trade unions resolved accordingly that the law must be changed, and scores of candidates at the general election pledged themselves to this effect. The bill eventually carried through parliament with the assent of both great parties restored the unions to the position they had occupied, with respect to trade disputes, in the thirty years before 1901, but it went further ; by declaring that no action should be brought against a trade union, whether of masters or men, for any tortious act—an immunity soon construed by the House of Lords to apply even when no trade dispute was in question—it apparently gave these bodies a wholly exceptional status of privilege in wrong-doing. Later on, in 1913, another Act, reversing another judicial decision, allowed a trade union to apply its funds to any lawful purpose, with the reservation that, if money was to be spent on political objects, a separate, and voluntary, fund must be maintained. Following on the recent grant of salaries to members of parliament, the effect of this Act was greatly to increase the chances of the Labour party.

Encouraged by the legislation of 1906 and by the trade boom then beginning, the unions widened their activities and aims, while they increased in numbers and wealth. Their leaders' thoughts turned from the mere improvement of working conditions, and even from the expulsion of non-union labour, towards schemes for the elimination of the capitalist and claims for a share in the control of industry. Strikes on a huge scale, intended to coerce employers through inconvenience caused to the community, now became common. A great railway strike, averted in 1907 by the government's offer of impartial conciliation boards, nevertheless broke out in 1911. In the same year the dockers and others employed at the Port of London turned out for better wages, and were in the main successful. The coal-miners, having secured an eight-hour day by Act of Parliament in 1908, struck nearly a million strong in 1912 in the greatest stoppage the country had then seen; to settle it the government rushed a bill through both Houses establishing the principle of a statutory minimum wage for underground workers. In 1914 the reorganized societies in these three industries — the railwaymen, the transport workers, and the miners—concluded a fighting alliance, but its strength was not put to the test. The total membership of all the unions at that date is estimated at about four millions; their power in the State had enormously increased and their co-operation, both individual and collective, was invited in great public enterprises.

The emergency Minimum Wage Act of 1912 was the extension, under duress, to a well-organized industry of a principle which had been first introduced three years before to rescue sweated workers at the other end of the scale. It was over a century since Whitbread had first proposed it in the days before *laissez-faire*, and now the wheel had come full circle. The application was narrow and tentative at first; only four ill-paid occupations came under the supervision of the new Trade Boards empowered to fix minimum rates of wages. At the end of the period a minimum wage for agricultural labourers was under consideration.

Many other laws of a collectivistic character were passed in these strenuous years for the protection of the weak. Mr. Balfour's Act of 1902 had made provision for public secondary schools, and education authorities were now permitted to feed necessitous school children at the ratepayers' charge, while special courts were set up to try child offenders. In 1908, weekly pensions were provided at the sole cost of the State for men and women over seventy. In 1911 a scheme, of German parentage, for the insurance of working men and women under the age of seventy against sickness was made compulsory, weekly contributions from employers and employed being supplemented by the State; in the case of certain trades insurance against unemployment was introduced on similar lines. By such measures it was hoped to lessen the material and moral loss to the nation occasioned by a vast expenditure on poor relief and by the treatment as paupers of people whose poverty might be due to no fault of their own.

It was a wonderful record of achievement, comparable with the legislative harvest of the early thirties, or the forties, or Gladstone's first ministry. Parliament had adopted the view that it is the duty of a civilized State actively to promote the welfare of its citizens at the common expense, drawing freely on the fortunes of the rich. In 1911 about 45 per cent. of the aggregate income of the population of the United Kingdom was received by rather more than a million persons and their families.[1] The effect of the Liberal legislation was in a slight degree to redress such inequality. Mr. Asquith's Budget

[1] Calculated from figures in Bowley, *Division of the Product of Industry*, 1919.

of 1907 taxed " unearned " more heavily than
" earned " incomes ; Mr. Lloyd George's, of
1909, introduced a " super-tax " on incomes
over £5,000, increased death-duties, and initiated
the taxation of land on new principles. In the
last year of the peace, when expenditure exceeded £200,000,000, about 60 per cent. of the
tax revenue was derived from direct, and 40
per cent. from indirect taxation. Eight years
before the proportions had been nearly equal.
Not unnaturally the Liberal fiscal policy was
resented by those who suffered from it, and the
Finance Bill of 1909 was rejected by the Lords.

For eighty years the shadow of the Upper
House had lain visibly across the path of Liberal
law-making. The shadow had deepened when
Gladstone first gave Liberalism a cutting edge.
In 1869, over the Irish Church, and in 1884, over
the redistribution of parliamentary seats, a
breach had been averted, partly by royal influence. In 1893 a Liberal Cabinet had acquiesced
in the rejection of an unpopular Home Rule bill,
though Gladstone's bold spirit had burned to
appeal to the country. From 1893 till 1906 the
Peers had slept, but now they were aggressively
awake. In their first years of power the Liberal
government had brought in an Education bill
intended to placate the English Nonconformists
chafing under the Anglican partiality, as they

considered it, of Mr. Balfour's Act of 1902 ; also bills dealing with land in Scotland, a bill abolishing plural voting, and a controversial Licensing bill. All these attacks on vested interests, having survived Conservative opposition in the Commons, were repulsed by the Conservative majority in the Lords, and the bills rejected. Then in 1909 the Peers filled up the cup, in the current phrase, by throwing out Mr. Lloyd George's Budget, which the custom of the constitution forbade them to amend. No Budget had been rejected by the Lords since finance bills of the modern type began in 1861, but Conservatives argued that the measure of 1909 contained items of far-reaching social importance, not merely financial in scope.

The Liberals were already pledged to clip the wings of the Lords, and welcoming the issue they dissolved parliament. Returned again to power, but with a greatly reduced majority and now dependent on the Irish vote, they secured their Budget and then introduced a bill limiting the powers of the Lords in ordinary legislation to a suspensory veto for two years. The course of events was delayed by the death of King Edward, but eventually, after a second general election which left the balance of power unchanged, the Parliament Bill became law in 1911. Liberals could now introduce controversial measures with some hope of putting them on the statute-book. Postponing the reform of the Upper House, they proceeded in 1912 to bring in a Home Rule bill for Ireland, a bill to disestablish and disendow the Anglican Church in Wales, and a Franchise bill extending the electorate from about seven and a half to ten millions and abolishing plural voting.

The 1909 Budget was swollen not only by provision for the new social services, but by largely increased expenditure on the navy. It was this which brought home to the ordinary man the growing tension in foreign relations. For in these years the vivid drama of home politics was running parallel to a vaster tragedy in world events, just as on the screen the pictures in two connected plots flash past in bewildering alternation, more and more closely interwoven as the story nears its catastrophe.

Experience in South Africa had shown how ill the country was equipped for the conduct of war. In 1903 a permanent Committee of Imperial Defence, including the professional heads of the fighting services, was constituted under the chairmanship of the Prime Minister to keep the defence policy of the Empire under constant supervision. Next, the War Office was reorganized at the top, and a real General Staff established for the first time. Then, in 1907, under Mr. Haldane's auspices, the army was re-modelled in prospect of possible service in a European war : an expeditionary force of six divisions formed the spear-point ; the militia became a Special Reserve to uphold it ; and in place of the Volunteers there was created the nucleus of a Territorial Force of fourteen divisions, primarily for home service. The Haldane reforms implied the rejection of the scheme for national military training advocated since 1905 by the veteran field-marshal, Lord Roberts, the most popular of living British soldiers ; though leaving the army deficient in important particulars, such as heavy artillery and machine guns, they immensely improved its efficiency and gave its several branches for the first time intelligible and mutually coherent functions. On the naval side the new orientation of defence policy was shown by the equipment of a naval base at Rosyth, on the east coast, in 1903 ; soon afterwards Lord Fisher almost recreated the navy as a fighting force, and the adoption of the *Dreadnought* type of battleship opened an era in shipbuilding, which now became definitely related to the growth of the German navy.

In all these developments the Dominions, so first officially styled at the Imperial Conference of 1907, were invited to play their part as allied nations exercising a free choice. But, illogically

enough, they had no say, except unofficially and
at intervals, in the formation of foreign policy,
for which Downing Street remained solely
responsible.

After the failure of the negotiations for a
German alliance, Mr. Balfour's government set
themselves to improve relations with France,
hitherto regarded, with her Russian ally, as
the natural enemy. An arbitration treaty was
followed in 1904 by the conclusion of the fateful
Entente, of which the chief definite feature was
a reciprocal undertaking by the two Powers to
give one another a free hand and diplomatic
support in Egypt and Morocco respectively.
The formal agreement came to be more and more
cordially ratified by public opinion, thanks partly
to King Edward's gracious diplomacy, partly to
growing fear of Germany. The Entente was not
considered in England as aimed against Germany; unfortunately the one issue—the Moroccan—in which it pledged British diplomatic
support to France was made critical by German
action within a few months, and so Anglo-
French friendship and Anglo-German friction
became associated in English minds.

The Moroccan crisis of 1905 was the first of
several in which the rulers of Germany, without
wishing to plunge the world in war, yet by a
course of blunders and bluster, due to bad

psychology and bad manners, to divided control and to downright incompetence, contrived to create in Europe the conviction that they did so. In this case the German Chancellor, taking up a controversy to which he had recently declared himself indifferent, and acting sometimes against the will, sometimes without the knowledge of the Kaiser, rejected the most conciliatory offers from France—whose conduct had indeed not been blameless—and induced her to dismiss the Foreign Minister who had negotiated the Entente. It would appear that Bülow had no object save to assert German " prestige " and a claim for territorial " compensations." But it is not surprising that such behaviour shook the Entente together, rather than apart ; nor that the leaders of the new Liberal government, following in their predecessors' steps, not only did not reject the possibility of giving France armed, as well as diplomatic, support, but authorized conversations to take place between the French and British General Staffs. At the same time, when the French ambassador asked if France could count on armed help from England in the event of a German attack, Sir Edward Grey, the Foreign Secretary, explained that no such assurance could be given ; England's decision must depend on the circumstances of the time. Yet in the minds of those who knew of these discussions—the majority of the Cabinet did not—the conception of the Entente must have somewhat developed; the Prime Minister himself felt a misgiving that something " very close to an honourable understanding " had arisen.

Russia's acceptance of defeat by the Japanese in 1905 was of profound importance in European no less than in Asiatic politics. As in the East it kindled a new self-confidence among Asiatic peoples, so it turned the energies of the rulers of Russia from the Far East to the Balkan peninsula, where friction with Germany's ally, Austria-Hungary, was almost unavoidable. And not with Austria only; since 1898 Germany herself, contrary to Bismarck's policy, had acquired interests of her own in the Turkish dominions, hoping that support of the Sultan would bear fruit in economic concessions. But the new western trend of Russian policy smoothed a way for the settlement of differences with England, for these were all in Asia. The Foreign Office no longer cared greatly to keep Russian warships out of the Straits. So Sir Edward Grey was able to negotiate a general understanding with Russia in 1907, Persia in this case filling the passive rôle allotted to Morocco and Egypt in the Anglo-French agreement. If England's settlement with France had been distasteful to Germany, that with Russia aroused her indignation. Here was England, a kindred Teutonic people, making an unnatural compact, aimed at the " encirclement " of Germany, with a barbaric Slavonic Power, whose armed millions were the nightmare of Germans small and great. To the greatest German of all it was particularly galling, since he had himself two years before concluded with the master of these barbaric millions a private—and abortive—treaty intended to destroy the Franco-Russian intimacy and isolate England.

The definite ranging of Russia on the side of the Entente made it seem imperative to Germany to run no risk of alienating her one secure ally, Austria-Hungary ; for in Italy she had little confidence. The centre of gravity of the Triple Alliance, it has been said, began to shift from Berlin to Vienna. Consequently when the next European crisis occurred, in 1908, as the result of a Balkan quarrel between Austria and Russia, Germany supported her ally without regard to the merits of the case, and at the risk of war.

All this counted as nothing to the ordinary Englishman beside the German challenge to British sea-power. Late in the nineties, when Germany had become a commercial and colonial power, a section of opinion, with which the young Kaiser had identified himself, demanded

that she should possess " a battle-fleet of such
a strength that, even for the most powerful
naval adversary, a war would involve such risks
as to make that Power's own supremacy doubtful." Such a fleet the Navy Law of 1900 proposed to give her; the Kaiser spoke of himself
in 1904 as Admiral of the Atlantic, and in 1906
and 1908 the building programme was increased.
This was the more disquieting that in 1906—
after the building of the *Dreadnought*—and in
1907 the British programme was actually
reduced. So after Germany had refused to
discuss the limitation of armaments publicly at
The Hague in 1907, and to discuss it confi-
dentially next year, the British government
decided in 1909 that a large increase was necessary, and public opinion became greatly excited.
It was natural, no doubt, for a colonial Power to
wish to possess a fleet, and for a proud empire to
wish to possess a strong fleet; but it was natural
also to realize that the richest country in Europe,
drawing four-fifths of its wheat supply from overseas, would never allow the strongest Continental
Power to possess a fleet that threatened its own.
In this case, unlike the Morocco episode, it was
the Kaiser himself who, following the advice of
Admiral Tirpitz, maintained an intransigent
attitude. " A good understanding with England," he wrote, " is not desirable at the cost

of the completion of Germany's fleet." For a country that really considered itself " encircled " such an attitude was madness.

Thus, like the hero of a Celtic myth who breaks one by one the spells that guard his welfare, Germany violated in turn all the canons of Bismarckian wisdom. She had allowed Russia to gravitate towards France : she had given hostages to fortune in the Balkans ; and now with open eyes she had antagonized England in a matter all Englishmen held vital.

In May 1909 Bethmann-Hollweg succeeded Bülow as German Chancellor ; like his predecessor, he wished to keep on good terms with England, but, being a weaker man, he was even less able to stand up to the Kaiser and Tirpitz, and he had no better idea of how to preserve peace. In the summer of 1911 the French were again active in Morocco ; the German government thought the occasion propitious for demanding large territorial compensations in Central Africa, and by way of showing that they meant business sent a gunboat without warning to the port of Agadir on the Moroccan coast. This disquieting gesture, as to which the silence of Germany and her contradictory explanations seemed equally ominous, brought the possibility of war nearer to the minds of Englishmen than ever before ; detailed plans were worked out for sending troops to the Continent in case of need. The tension passed, but the impression remained; while Mr. Winston Churchill was sent to the Admiralty to put the fleet in instant readiness for war, Admiral Tirpitz won the Kaiser's consent to a supplementary navy bill adding greatly to Germany's striking power.

"During all this period," Lord Grey has written, "whenever we seemed to be in sight of improved relations with Germany, we were thrown back by the continued expansion of the German fleet." A final attempt was now made to end the disastrous rivalry. But in vain; for it was soon evident that, while to the British it was a question of, if possible, getting the *old* navy law reduced in return for colonial support for Germany, coupled with a promise to join in no aggressive action against her, the Germans would only offer modifications of the *new* navy bill in return for a promise of neutrality amounting virtually to a renunciation of the Entente. Germany was to keep her allies and add to her fleet, while England was to return to her old uncomfortable isolation.

So the new naval programme, save for one ship, became law; Mr. Churchill's truism that for Germany a fleet was a luxury, while for England it was a necessity, was received with indignation in Berlin; and his suggestion of a year's naval " holiday " with scorn. On the British side it was decided to keep a 60 per cent. superiority over capital ships built under the old navy law, while building two keels to every one built under the new. A programme of oil-burning battleships was laid down, faster and more heavily gunned than any hitherto designed, and the naval estimates rose in 1914 to over 52 millions. Meanwhile, to concentrate strength in home waters, all battleships were temporarily withdrawn from the Mediterranean. The French fleet was concentrated there for the same reason, and discussions took place between the two Admiralties on this basis ; in 1914 naval conversations were authorized with Russia. As the sense of danger increased, it was inevitable that Britain should look on the other Powers of the Entente more and more as potential allies and be anxious not to estrange them. Perhaps this development increased the danger. But no obligations of common action in case of war were undertaken, and letters were in fact exchanged between Sir Edward Grey and the French ambassador in November 1912 to make the situation clear.

The failure of the naval discussions, following on the Agadir crisis, diminished the hope among Englishmen conversant with foreign affairs that peace could be long maintained. The Emperor and his Chancellor might desire it, but there loomed behind them malign influences which, if they were not planning war, yet seemed to regard the risk of it as a normal incident of politics. To understand the prevalent fear of Germany's intentions it is not enough to study the policies and methods now disclosed in her archives ; it is necessary to picture her vast military, commercial and industrial strength, her youthful energy and confident ambitions ; to picture also the immense and obtrusive prestige of the army and its leaders, the tradition of Prussian discipline, and the talk of eminent Germans, from the Kaiser downwards, about sharp swords and shining armour and Germany's future upon the water. It seemed incredible to Englishmen that this steel-girt empire could really fear aggression from a nation of shopkeepers, whose best European customer she was, and whose commerce depended upon peace ; or from France, on whose soil a war would probably be fought and whose people remembered the horrors such war involved. Of Russia Englishmen knew little ; they thought of her as lately battered in war and torn by revolution, far less well equipped than Germany for a modern campaign. Yet Germany did fear her two great neighbours, and watched with the utmost suspicion the relations between them and England. She was aware of the naval and military conversations and could see that France had denuded her northern and western coasts of warships. She believed that these measures meant more than was the case, and that England was in fact the ally of France and Russia, bound in the last resort to view matters as they did.

The British government have been blamed for not taking the nation into their confidence in these years, so soon as the failure of the naval discussions was apparent, and preparing it for the imminence of war. But they still hoped for peace, and feared to take any step which might provoke German hostility. In point of fact, relations with Germany decidedly improved in the next two years, as the result of joint efforts to keep the Balkan wars from spreading, and of the conclusion of important agreements touching the future of the Portuguese colonies and the Bagdad railway. In the summer of 1914 the prospects of peace were brighter than they had been for many months.

The welcome lull in foreign affairs did not extend to events at home. The last years of the armed peace were an epoch of almost unexampled strain and strife in the United Kingdom. Stoppages on an increasing scale were becoming a normal feature of industrial life. The agitation for female suffrage was conducted on the part of a section of women with extreme acerbity venting itself in the destruction of property and other violent acts. But it was from the factiousness of the political parties that the gravest dangers impended. The elections of 1900 and 1906 had bequeathed a cup of bitterness, to which the rival education bills added drops of sectarian venom. The Lloyd George Budget, and its author's invective, had aroused intense indignation among the classes with property, and particularly among landowners, so long predominant in social and political power. The resistance of the Lords, and the government's use of the royal prerogative to break it, had merged the economic issue in the constitutional. Now the religious quarrel was renewed by the bill for Welsh disestablishment; a drastic reorganization of the whole system of land tenure was threatened, and, worst of all, the Home Rule issue had risen from the tomb.

In 1821 the population of Ireland was three times that of Scotland. In 1901 it was less than that of Scotland, and it was still dwindling. But Ireland no longer suffered from such neglect as had prevailed before the seventies. The resolute Unionist government inaugurated by Mr. Balfour in the eighties had not only restored order, but had begun relief measures, had stimulated agriculture, and had so widely extended

the system of State-aided land purchase that
nearly half the soil now belonged to the tenants.
From the Liberals Ireland had received a Roman
Catholic university and her share of old age
pensions and insurance. But the demand of the
Catholic population for autonomy had survived
Parnell and survived the grant of elected County
Councils; the Central Council offered as an
instalment by the Liberals in 1907 had been
rejected, and now the Nationalist party, holding
the balance in the Commons, called on the
Liberals to carry out the policy to which Glad-
stone had dedicated them a generation before.

The Liberals believed the spirit of the time
was with them. In 1906, only four years after
the Boer war, Campbell-Bannerman had taken
the daring step of giving full responsible government to the Transvaal and Orange River Colony.
So well had this policy succeeded that in 1909
the two Boer communities joined with Cape
Colony and Natal to form the Union of South
Africa, ranking with the Dominion of Canada,
the Commonwealth of Australia, and New Zealand, as a self-governing nation under the British
Crown. In 1911 Louis Botha, ten years before
a Boer general, now Prime Minister of the Union,
took part in the councils of the Empire as a member of the Imperial Conference. But Liberal
statesmen had pushed even further their leader's

maxim that good government is no substitute for self-government. The germs of nationalist and democratic aspiration had appeared in India; minds indoctrinated with English political philosophy had thrilled to the Japanese victories over a Western Power, and to the constitutionalist revolution in Turkey. Wishing to show sympathy with these ideas, yet profoundly conscious of the significance of the change, Lord Morley and Lord Minto introduced an elected element into the Indian Legislative Councils and appointed Indian members to the Council of India in London and even to the Viceroy's Council in India.

More complicated than the South African problem or the Indian, and apparently insoluble on federal lines, the issue of Home Rule was embittered by past memories and unceasing distrust. From the outset the government were guilty of one capital blunder; they wholly misgauged the force of Ulster's determination to resist Home Rule, which differed utterly from the ordinary obstructiveness of a parliamentary opposition. It was rooted in something deeper than reason, in solid conviction formed by close on three centuries of religious fear and racial pride. It is strange that the Cabinet should not have foreseen that in 1914, if not earlier, they would be faced by three alternatives: to drop their Home Rule bill, to exclude Ulster, or to coerce her. They preferred to wait on events, doing nothing to discourage the belief that Ulster would be brought under the yoke of Dublin by armed force. Their difficulties were greatly increased by the need of conciliating the Nationalists, who by voting against them could put them in a minority. Nor were the Nationalists themselves free agents : a Separatist group, eager to supplant them, watched from Ireland for any sign of truckling to the Saxon oppressor.

The cumbrous procedure of the Parliament Act, which doomed the Home Rule bill to be three times alternately passed by the Commons and rejected by the Lords, gave the Ulster Unionists plenty of time to organize resistance. Led by Sir Edward Carson, a former law-officer of the Crown, they held monster meetings and solemnly covenanted, under the auspices of religion, to withstand Home Rule to the last. They drilled, they imported arms, and finally they formed a Provisional Government against the day when the bill should be enforced. Ulster cared nothing for English and Scottish opinion and was prepared to resist to all eternity. But the Unionists of Great Britain would not follow to that length. Claiming that the country had never been consulted on the issue, they pledged themselves, under Mr. Bonar Law's leadership, to support whatever measures the Ulstermen should take, unless and until Home Rule should be sanctioned by a general election or a referendum. One or other of these two they moved heaven and earth to obtain.

The raising of troops in Ulster naturally provoked a counter-movement in the South, and by the spring of 1914 two armed Volunteer forces, neither under the control of the Crown, faced one another on Irish soil. But what of the forces of the Crown itself ? Towards the end of March the country was compelled to think what a deadlock would mean in practice by the action of certain army officers at the Curragh, who offered to resign their commissions rather than take part in the coercion of Ulster. Their action was, apparently, based on a misunderstanding of what the government required of them, but the incident was wider in its bearings than the issue of Irish Home Rule. It forced to the front, at a time of heated passions, the whole question of the limits of the State's right to demand obedience from its members, civilian as well as military. If an officer might refuse to serve against Ulster, must a soldier feel bound to obey orders in case of a trade dispute ? The case was a practical one, for in 1911 the Government had not shrunk from the thought of using troops to secure the national food supply and to overawe the railwaymen on strike. And at this very moment scores of women were justifying arson and other crimes by the plea that they were denied the suffrage.

Meanwhile all attempts to find an agreed settlement about Ulster had broken down. In March, a few days before the Curragh incident, the government had offered to exclude any county which so voted from the Home Rule bill for six years ; so that no question of " coercion " could arise till after two general elections. The Opposition demanded that the exclusion should be permanent, and negotiations continued till the end of July, when the Buckingham Palace Conference ended in a dispute between the two Irish parties as to whether the whole, or parts only, of two Ulster counties should be excluded. The breakdown was symbolic of the narrowness of view shown by the principals on both sides alike.

In political circles there was now intense excitement, and the peace of Ireland seemed to hang by a thread. How far the mass of the people of Great Britain was really stirred it is difficult to say. The working classes were more interested by the movement of events in industry, and country folk by Mr. Lloyd George's land proposals, while the conduct of the militant suffragists had inured men's minds to violence.

The last three years and more had been a nightmare of passion and paradox :—Liberals planning to force a hated yoke on Ulster, Conservatives and " loyalists " rehearsing rebellion, officers demanding guarantees from the War Office, employers and workmen losing millions of pounds in industrial strife, educated women setting fire to houses and churches. Statesmanship was bankrupt, and the authority of the State, already challenged in Syndicalist theory, seemed to be collapsing in sober fact. Such was the situation when the knot which the politicians could not untie was cut by the sword, and the sternest of schoolmasters retaught the lessons of unity and discipline.

CHAPTER XI

It would be useless to summarize in a few pages the course of the tremendous conflict which began for the British Empire on August 4, 1914, and ended on November 11 four long years later. But it may be possible to indicate some of the ways in which it influenced the life of the nation.

It was the German invasion of Belgium, and the Belgian appeal for British help, which brought Cabinet, parliament and people almost unanimously into the war. Yet after the events of recent years it would have been impossible for England long to remain neutral and allow France to be crushed in a war not of her own seeking; and it seemed clear then, as it seems much clearer now, that the war was forced by the reckless impetuosity of the rulers of Austria-Hungary, unrestrained and indeed encouraged at the critical time by the rulers of Germany. As in 1909, Germany gave her " last ally " a free hand in a Balkan quarrel, and Austria snatched at an opportunity to destroy once for all the Serbian hopes of detaching her Southern Slav provinces. Stronger than in 1909, Russia would not again fail the Serbs in their extremity, and after Austria had declared war on Serbia the hope of confining the struggle to the Balkans was slight. On both sides military considerations acquired fatal force ; the precipitate Russian mobilization led Germany also to mobilize, and on August 1 the European war began.

Once the peace was broken and the floodgates of fear, falsehood, and hatred opened, there was small chance of an ending until one or other side was exhausted. Indeed, the scale and intensity of the conflict increased month by month, and Britain's use of her sea-power involved her in acute controversy with the United States. From the winter of 1916 onwards there was talk of a negotiated peace, but not till after their front had been broken in France in August 1918 were the Central Powers ready to offer terms which there was any likelihood of the Allies accepting. By then all the German colonies had been conquered, Syria and Mesopotamia were slipping from the grasp of the Turks, Russia had dissolved in Communism, and the United States had an army fighting in France.

Meanwhile the life of the British people had

been transformed. The unsleeping watch of the navy and the heroism of the tiny force, which in the retreat from Mons, on the Marne, and at Ypres helped France to repel the German onset, gave a respite for their country to organize itself for a long war. Such catchwords as " business as usual " became ridiculous when the nation was facing imminent danger of military defeat, financial collapse, or actual starvation ; it survived only by accepting startling changes in its political and economic traditions. In the process State and individual citizen alike revealed remarkable powers of enduring unprecedented strains and adapting themselves to unforeseen emergencies. This revelation was one of the chief lessons of the war.

As the hopes of peace faded in July 1914, the controversies between the British parties, between Nationalists and Ulstermen, Labour and Capital, the women and the law, promptly subsided, and a single spirit of co-operation ruled. So little had the implications of a European war been realized in England that, after the Grand Fleet had moved to its war-station in the Orkneys, the Territorials been embodied, and the Expeditionary Force concentrated in Flanders, everything else was improvisation. In the first place an army on a Continental scale had to be raised and maintained, and in order to equip it for trench warfare munitions were urgently required in quantities hitherto inconceivable. The supply of these needs alone involved the most drastic inroads on the liberty and welfare of the individual.

It was at once clear that, if munitions were to be forthcoming as required, the usual trade union conditions concerning hours and the recruitment of labour must be waived in the industries affected. The unions were naturally reluctant to surrender their hardly won charters of liberties without making certain that these would eventually be restored and that the nation would reap the full benefit of the sacrifice. The Munitions Act of 1915 was based on an agreement between the government and the trade union leaders, but it gave openings for complaints on the part of the men, of whom many were dissatisfied with the concessions their leaders were making : while only to some extent limiting private profits in " controlled " factories, it enabled the Minister to suspend any trade restriction, imposed compulsory arbitration and prohibited strikes, and went a long way towards binding a workman to his occupation. Later on, State-owned shell factories were started, and in the course of the war both the railways and the mines were subjected to State control. Yet strikes occurred, of which the notable feature was their unofficial character, the shop-stewards in individual works heading an opposition to the trade union executives. The great majority of workmen, however, whose friends and brothers were on service, discountenanced the strikes, and the vast output of munitions in the later months of the war bore witness to their patriotism.

The supply of munitions was delayed by the enlistment of many skilled workmen in the army. The early rush to the Colours had been magnificent, but many recruits taken would have been more useful at their civilian jobs, and in time the stream dried up. By the beginning of 1916 it was agreed that only conscription could keep the army at the necessary strength, and the first of several Military Service Acts was passed. It, like the Munitions Act, was approved by the official spokesmen of Labour and the great majority of their followers.

A further wide extension of State interference resulted from the German attempt to cut off the nation's supplies by submarine warfare. By the end of 1916 the rate at which merchantmen were sunk was rising so fast as to cause grave anxiety, and the Lloyd George government, with ultimate success, took vigorous measures to stimulate the home production, reduce the consumption, and organize the distribution of necessaries. The cultivation of land was controlled by local committees with statutory authority; farmers in return were guaranteed standard prices and fixed rents, while minimum wage rates were set for labourers. Retail prices were fixed for essential foodstuffs, and ration-cards limited the amount of them a single person might buy. No such regard for the poor had been shown in the food shortage of a century before.

The war affected every family in the country no less directly through the prodigious rise in the cost of living, due, in the main, to the immense purchases of the government, which involved a large inflation of the currency. In order to meet its infinite requirements and those of its Allies, the government not only increased taxation and borrowed insatiably from the public and from America, but hugely expanded the currency by borrowing from the banks and from the Bank of England and by issuing Treasury notes practically inconvertible into gold. By the end of the war over 780 millions were being raised by taxation towards an expenditure of nearly 3,000 millions, the national debt had soared from 650 to nearly 7,500 millions, and wholesale prices stood more than 130 per cent. higher than in July 1914. For working-class families the rise in prices was moderated by government control in items chiefly concerning them, such as bread, meat, and rent; but by the end of the war the amount of an average budget had more than doubled. On the other hand, unemployment had disappeared; a great part of the male population was being well fed and clothed in the army; wages had risen nearly, if not quite, as high as the cost of living, and large classes at home, especially women, girls, and boys, which had not previously contributed to the family income, were now earning high wages and spending freely. As against this there was a growing shortage of houses, and the long hours of exacting, monotonous work left little leisure; but these very hours obliged employers to study how factory conditions could be made most favourable to efficiency, and to provide opportunities for rest and relaxation.

The good wages earned by munition workers tended along with other factors to the blurring of class distinctions. Working girls off duty dressed as smartly as women of any other class, just as by the end of the war officers' uniform was worn by young men of all classes alike, whereas large numbers of Public School boys were serving, or had served, in the ranks. On the other hand, many families dependent on fixed incomes were forced by the rise in prices, and by income tax at five or six shillings in the pound, to abandon their old style of living, while swarms of government contractors and lucky investors rose to affluence. On the lives of women in particular the changes of these years had a revolutionary effect. Women and girls of all classes were called upon to do men's work in the factories, in the fields, as public officials and as drivers of cars and lorries. Drawing good pay and often living away from home, they acquired a new sense of independence and power of initiative. So too millions of men who joined the army were introduced to an entirely strange form of existence, and incidentally a much greater proportion of the people than ever before saw life outside their native islands. In the Flanders mud, on the Gallipoli beaches, in all the many theatres of war, they mixed with men of different experiences and revised their scale of values.

A government confronted with the infinite emergencies of such a war could not fail to arouse, and to deserve, criticism, and in time, despite political truce and censorship, criticism was sure to express itself forcibly. Reconstructed on a coalition basis in May 1915, Mr. Asquith's government gave place in December 1916 to that of Mr. Lloyd George, whose energy in providing munitions had marked him for leadership. The supreme direction of the war was now committed to a small War Cabinet, to which the departmental Ministers—in several cases business or professional men without parliamentary experience—were summoned only when specially concerned. But the concentration of attention on the work of winning the war did not prevent the passing in 1918 of two agreed political measures of the highest importance; together they seemed to recognize that expansion of individual capacity, actual and potential, of which events had given proof. The widest Reform bill of British history raised the numbers of the electorate to twenty millions, of which six millions were calculated to be women, and a new scope and impulse were given by Mr. Fisher's bill to educational policy. In the previous year Mr. Whitley's committee initiated a movement for improving industrial relations, by recommending the formation of Joint Councils to enable representatives of employers and organized labour to discuss matters affecting their common welfare.

Imperial questions also were treated with a generous breadth of view. It was recognized that the part played by the Dominions in the war entitled them to the full status of nationhood. The services and aspirations of India were not less clamant. Consequently the Imperial War Conference of 1917, while postponing

" the readjustment of the constitutional relations
of the component parts of the Empire " till after
the war, pronounced the opinion that any such
readjustment " should be based on a full recognition of the Dominions as autonomous nations
of an Imperial Commonwealth, and of India
as an important portion of the same, should
recognize the right of the Dominions and India
to an adequate voice in foreign policy and in
foreign relations, and should provide effective
arrangements for continuous consultation in all
important matters of common Imperial concern
and for such necessary concerted action, founded
on consultation, as the several Governments
may determine." And the imperial parliament
pledged itself to the policy " of the increasing
association of Indians in every branch of the
[Indian] administration and the gradual development of self-governing institutions with a view
to the progressive realization of responsible
government in India as an integral part of the
British Empire."

In Ireland the record was less happy. The
popularity of the Nationalist party, which supported the war and reluctantly consented to
concessions to Ulster, was gradually undermined
by the Sinn Fein separatists with their more
adventurous slogan of an Irish republic.
Favoured by the astonishing apathy of the

British authorities, the Sinn Fein leaders organized a rebellion with German help, and at Easter, 1916, an armed insurrection broke out in Dublin. The rising was suppressed and fifteen ringleaders executed, but the Sinn Fein organization was allowed to revive, and in 1918 it was sweeping the country. The breakdown of the Dublin Convention that spring marked the failure of the last attempt to settle the Irish question by agreement, and the extent of the failure was measured by the fact that not even when the need was sorest did the government dare to conscript the manhood of Ireland or to ration her food.

The advocates of Irish independence could appeal to the fashionable doctrine of national self-determination. Out of the declarations of the belligerent governments, the dogmas of the Russian Bolsheviks, the speeches of President Wilson, and the thoughts of men and women everywhere disillusioned with war and the rampant nationalism which had produced it, there was emerging a new gospel of international morality. In 1918 it won general lip-service. The official war aims stated by Mr. Lloyd George in January were hardly distinguishable from those fathered by the Labour party, and a Foreign Office committee was at work in the spring on the draft constitution of a League of

Nations. This idea, dimly apprehended a century before by Castlereagh and the Tsar Alexander, had been welcomed in the autumn of 1914 by Mr. Asquith and Sir Edward Grey; it had since been authoritatively preached by President Wilson, and four years of inter-allied co-operation now gave it a basis of practical experience as the latest methods of warfare gave it a new urgency.

By the summer of 1918 the Germans had shot their bolt. Before their last terrific onslaught the Allied armies had reeled but not broken. Their submarines had been mastered, while they themselves were suffering cruelly from the Allied blockade. Backed by the inexhaustible American reserves, the Allied forces in France at length took the initiative, and events moved swiftly and suddenly to the crowning mercy of the Armistice.

Over the greater part of Europe the war had lowered the standard of well-being for a long time to come and had removed thousands of those best fitted to lead the thought of mankind. Old restraints had perished with old ways of life, and in many minds confusion reigned. Let us eat and drink, for to-morrow we die, had seemed a natural creed. But the war had not killed European civilization, nor yet the vitality of the British peoples; much that had blocked progress had been swept away, and in the two dark danger zones of industrial and international relations ideas offering some hope for the future had recently shone out.

CHAPTER XII

THE hopes of peace and prosperity inspired by the Allied victory were not fulfilled. The "war to end wars" had in fact aroused explosive forces of nationalism which the peace settlement did not assuage, and so far was the world from being made "safe for democracy" that relations between classes and countries were poisoned by totalitarian doctrines, communist or fascist, which scorned the idea of liberty and in their cruel intolerance recalled the religious fanaticism of the past. Within twenty years a yet more destructive war was to convulse the world; in the meantime it was long before it recovered from the ravages of the last. Only for a few years at the end of the 'twenties did the sky clear. If Britain suffered less than other countries from economic disturbance, she had been brought near enough to the Continent by the conquest of the air to have lost her island security.

In the world of thought, revolutionary concepts of the nature of the universe were formed by astronomers and physicists. Einstein's theories of relativity, Rutherford's work on the structure of the atom, the mysteries of quantum mechanics, could be understood only by the few; but the writings of such men as Whitehead, Jeans and Eddington made the ordinary man realise that traditional beliefs were out of date. Advances in applied science, on the other hand, ministered in marvellous ways to his convenience and interest, particularly in transportation and communications. In this period motor vehicles went far to banish the horse from the roads, the farms and the army; travel by air became common; the cinema, first silent, later with sound, became the successful rival of the theatre; while the wireless or radio, entering millions of homes, extended the possibilities of amusement, education and propaganda and as a medium of information challenged the monopoly of the Press. In matters of welfare, great attention was devoted to nutrition, largely owing to the discovery of vitamins; the clearance of slums and overcrowded areas was accepted as a public responsibility.

Longevity was increasing, but the falling birthrate pointed to a society in which the older age groups would predominate, and eventually to a stationary population. In the United Kingdom of 1931 in a total of 46 millions females exceeded males by nearly two millions, and consequently formed the majority of the electorate after adult suffrage was introduced in 1928. An Act of 1919 had removed most of the legal disqualifications attaching to women.

Generally speaking, the reaction, conspicuous before the war, against Victorian standards in taste and conduct continued. Manners and dress were less formal; divorces increased. The doctrines of Freud and Jung were widely known and accepted, throwing a strange new light on the working of the human mind and the nature of personality. The flight from institutional religion also continued, but agnosticism was less militant and among religious bodies there was a greater desire for mutual understanding. The long schism between the Established and Free branches of the Scottish Presbyterian Kirk was healed in 1924; the creation of a National Assembly in 1919 gave laymen a larger part in the affairs of the Church of England, but the dependence of the Church on state control was shown in the rejection of the Revised Prayer Book in 1928.

The disillusionment and perplexity of the period appeared in much of its literature. T. S. Eliot's *Waste Land* (1922) was typical in this respect and in its rejection of traditional form. The poems of Gerard Manley Hopkins, only recently published, had also a strong influence. Literature in fact entered on a revolutionary phase, as did the visual arts: the realistic sculpture of Epstein, like the novels of D. H. Lawrence, showed a conscious revolt against all that the Victorians had admired. On the other hand a series of winter exhibitions at Burlington House gave opportunities of appreciating masterpieces representing the traditional art of many countries. The cheap press continued to specialize in sensational matter, largely crime, sex and disasters; however, cheap paper-backed editions of books old and new encouraged serious reading and the wireless spread an appreciation of good music.

Since the outbreak of the war, which had dislocated the orderly economic life of Western Europe accustomed to comparatively stable price-levels and foreign exchanges, the nations had been living from hand to mouth. Production and transportation had been directed to immediate purposes without count of cost; an orgy of spending had resulted in vast inflation. The return to "normalcy," in President Harding's phrase, proved a slow and painful process. Large areas of the world were impoverished; overproduction was general; each country was tempted to pursue its own obvious ends without regard to repercussions outside.

Britain had not suffered from devastation, loss of territory or political upheaval, but as a country which depended largely on foreign trade she was hard hit. In particular the blow fell on her old staple exporting industries—coal, iron and steel, textiles, shipbuilding and shipping. For some of them the future was dark, for their distress was not due only to the war. As a century earlier, the war aggravated tendencies already apparent. From the seventies British pre-eminence in industry and technology was declining, overtaken by competitors who had started later. The process had gone on, and countries hitherto economically important mainly as primary producers, such as Canada and India, were now fostering manufactures of their own. Lancashire cotton was one of the chief sufferers. Coal, moreover, was challenged by oil and hydro-electric power, iron by lighter metals; and now that distant parts of the globe were being opened up by the internal-combustion engine there was less demand for locomotives. These changes would have taken place even without a war, while the sad plight of agriculture, no longer favoured as in wartime, was nothing new.

But over and above the inevitable consequences of five years of war the return to prosperity was blocked by two artificial hindrances—reparations and war debts. The natural desire of the victors to recover as much as possible of the material losses they had suffered in a war for which they held Germany responsible had led them in 1919 to impose on the vanquished the obligation to pay immense sums in kind and in cash over a long period of years; acrimonious bickerings had followed as to the method of payment and the distribution of the proceeds between the Allies. On the other hand the Continental Allies had incurred to Britain, and the European Allies generally had incurred to the United States, for the purposes of the war huge debts which they were now due to repay. The sums involved were far too large to settle by transfers of gold, whereas in the case of debts owing to America payment in goods was barred by the American tariff wall. To the Europeans, who had suffered so much worse and so much longer than the Americans, it seemed unfair that these commitments incurred in the common cause should be treated as commercial debts. But they had promised to pay, and the manner in which some of them spent such revenues as they possessed did not incline Congress to let them off. The British did, in fact, by the Balfour note of August 1922, offer to reduce their claims on the Continentals by the amount that the United States would reduce her claims on Britain. But the United States did not favour the suggestion, and the two nuisances of Reparations and War Debts bedevilled international relations until both were jettisoned in the economic cataclysm of the thirties. For long after it the British default rankled in American minds.

A short after-war boom was followed in Britain by several years of depression. But despite the decline in our export industries and the consequent adverse balance of trade, despite vastly increased expenditure to cover swollen debt charges and social services, British governments, unlike those of most European countries, balanced their budgets by dint of heavy taxation. Industrial efficiency was increased, not always without legislative compulsion, and not always to the extent required, by the amalgamation of concerns and by other forms of "rationalization." And, while the old staple industries languished, some others less dependent on overseas markets were flourishing: such were aircraft and automobile construction, electrical engineering, the production of rayon and plastics, and the building and distributive trades. The national income rose, though overseas investments never reached the level of 1914. Progressive taxation—income tax, surtax and estate duty—refashioned yet further the pattern of society, but it has been calculated that in 1936 one-half of the property privately owned, in England and Wales, was in the hands of 1 per cent. of the population aged over 25.[1]

From the point of view of the working classes, the period as a whole is remembered as one of disillusionment and degradation, and so it was in the case of thousands of families in certain industries and certain areas. The men returning from the trenches had been promised "homes for heroes," whereas there was a shortage of some 800,000 houses and large slum and overcrowded areas cried out for reconstruction. Workers at home had hoped to maintain and improve upon the high wages and shorter hours they had won, and resented and resisted the efforts of employers hit by the slump to reduce costs at their expense. But if wages fell so did the cost of living, and for the working population as a whole it seems that, while real wages were falling from 1920 to 1922, they were rising for the next ten years and were stationary from 1932 to 1937.[2] A summary comparison with pre-war figures suggests that "average earnings had just about doubled since 1914, while the cost of living had risen by only 55 per cent.; hence the standard of living of the

[1] Taken from Court's *Concise Economic History of Britain* (1954) pp. 109–10, citing H. Campion, *Public and Private Property in Great Britain* (1939), p. 299; one sixth of the total property was owned or directly administered by public bodies.

[2] Layton and Crowther, *Introduction to the Study of Prices* (1938 edn.).

average employed worker was about 30 per cent. higher in 1937 than before the war." [1]

But averages are bloodless things, and a terribly high proportion of the people was not employed. This was the most deplorable fact about these twenty years at home, and that which left the deepest scar in the memories of the workers. Throughout the whole period the unemployment figures never dropped much below a million, and at the worst time, in 1932, they reached nearly three millions. As a percentage of insured workers for the years 1921–37 they averaged over 14 per cent., never less than 10 per cent. and in 1931–2 over 20 per cent., while in some industries they were far higher. For unemployment was by no means spread evenly over the country, and it is easy therefore to form a distorted view. It was worst, and chronic, in the industries and areas dependent on the export trade—South Wales, the Clyde, north-eastern and north-western England. These districts, for which no future on traditional lines could be seen when pits or mills or dockyards closed, became known as Depressed or Special Areas; except in so far as new enterprises could be started in them migration to happier districts seemed the only remedy, and there was

[1] Jones and Pool, *A Hundred Years of Economic Development* (1940).

in fact a considerable shift of population to Greater London and the midland and southern counties, reversing the trend of a century earlier.

In former days the unemployed would have been left to the mercies of the Poor Law, but by 1920 national insurance on a contributory basis covered unemployment in nearly all industries except agriculture and domestic service. The scheme, however, had never envisaged such extensive or prolonged unemployment as now prevailed, and its actuarial basis collapsed. It was therefore necessary to provide funds—known as uncovenanted or extended benefit or, more popularly, the dole—to meet the needs of those who had exhausted their rights under the scheme. Eventually, in 1934, an Unemployment Assistance Board was set up to provide for these cases, but throughout the period controversy raged as to the proper scales and conditions of relief. Successive governments were deeply concerned with this intractable problem, but none found a solution. Such public works as were started were on too small a scale to be of much good. The possibility of maintaining full employment by state manipulation of currency and investment was as yet a dream of a few economists, of whom the most eminent was J. M. Keynes.

The early years after the war were a time of

bitter industrial strife.   This was a legacy from
the years before it, but the interval had suggested
new ideas and raised fresh hopes.   The influence
of the Russian revolution must not be discounted.
Communism as such made little appeal to
Englishmen—it never secured more than one or
two seats in the House of Commons—but the
triumph of working men in one great country
could not fail to stir the imagination of their
fellows all over the world, and in Britain trade
unionism at the end of the war was strong and
militant.   Strikes and lock-outs were common—
notably in the coal industry, where they were
almost chronic, in cotton and on the railways,
though these last were a "sheltered" industry,
not exposed to foreign competition.   But in the
prevailing depression the men fought at a disadvantage and the time was not ripe for united
action. The Triple Alliance of railwaymen,
transport workers and miners broke down in
1921, and the General Strike of May 1926, called
by the General Council of the Trade Union Council
in support of the miners, failed after nine days
in face of national disapproval and efficient
counter-organization.   Its failure and the doubtful constitutional points raised by it discouraged
any further such demonstration on the part of
labour and later years were more peaceful.   The
membership of the unions dropped from over

eight millions in 1920 to less than four-and-a-half in 1933, after which it began to recover.

In spite of all this there were ups as well as downs in the national economy. From 1924 it seemed that revival had fairly begun. Next year income tax was reduced to 4s., the lowest level reached in this period, and the government decided to restore the gold standard. Gold coins had disappeared for good from circulation during the war, but for international purposes notes were now made convertible with gold, unfortunately at the old parity. The pound, it was said, could now look the dollar in the face again. But it soon became clear that the pound was overvalued, with disastrous results for our struggling export trades in the next six years.

The recovery did not last beyond 1929. The New York financial crash of that year started a chain reaction in the European economy, causing utter collapse of credit and confidence on the Continent. In Britain in 1931 heavy government spending prophesied a huge deficit in the budget, and the calling in of short-term loans by foreigners threatened to denude the Bank of England of gold and consequently to drive the country off the gold standard. This, if done when the credit of the nation was good, as in fact occurred soon afterwards, might be all for the best, but to be forced off gold as things stood was at any cost to be avoided. Drastic economies were agreed to be necessary, but the majority of the Labour Cabinet could not bring themselves to authorize the cuts in unemployment benefit without which it was very widely held impossible to balance the budget and restore the national credit. Thereupon the Prime Minister, Ramsay MacDonald, resigned, to form an all-party National Government prepared to cope with the situation. They did not in fact save the pound—exaggerated stories of a "mutiny" in the Fleet renewed the lack of confidence abroad—but they balanced the budget and, after being confirmed in power by the electorate with an enormous majority over the Labour opposition, proceeded to introduce various innovations of a far-reaching character. Not content with tentative and partial defensive measures they enacted in 1932 a system of full-blooded protection; they followed this up by negotiating an interchange of Imperial preferences at Ottawa and bilateral commercial treaties with foreign countries. In the same year they carried through a successful conversion loan, and money remained cheap for the rest of the period. The cuts in salaries and unemployment benefit were restored by 1935 and the economy continued to improve. Subsidies and quotas brought relief to certain industries, but no remedy was found for "the hard core" of unemployment in others, and the Labour Party, which had repudiated MacDonald, never relaxed its animosity for what it regarded as his betrayal.

During nearly the whole of this time the Conservatives were the largest party in the Commons, though the government might call itself Coalition (till 1922) or National (from 1931). Conservative distrust of Lloyd George broke up the wartime Coalition and the Liberal party never held office again. Only in 1924 and 1929–31 was Labour in office; it was never in power, for not having an absolute majority it governed by sufferance of the other two parties. The Liberals' small numbers in the House did not accord with either their strength in the country or their individual talents. Their frustration was due partly to personal feuds or differences of opinion between the followers of Asquith and Lloyd George, of Samuel and Simon, partly to their inability to put forward a distinctive programme. But neither were the other parties free from divisions; in both of them the cleavage of opinion between the extreme and the moderate wing was more noticeable than that between the moderates of each. Indeed the leaders of each, Ramsay MacDonald and Stanley Baldwin, had much of the Liberal in them. MacDonald, the creator of the Labour Party, became more and more out of touch with its more radical members, while Baldwin's main motive in entering politics was to heal class bitterness; in his handling of the Abdication crisis he represented the views of the great majority of all parties. Neville Chamberlain, who succeeded him, was of a more provocative spirit, but he too, as a skilled municipal administrator, was eager to promote social reform; protection, the distinctive Conservative policy, was advocated largely as a cure for unemployment.[1]

The popularity of the monarchy was demonstrated at George V's Silver Jubilee in 1935. Great things were hoped of the Prince of Wales, who succeeded him as Edward VIII. But the peoples of the Empire could not reconcile the new King's determination to marry a lady who had two former husbands living with the standards set by his parents, and the sympathy felt for his brother, who with his Scottish consort assumed the unwelcome burden in December 1936 as George VI, was soon to turn to admiration and affection.

The equal national status of the great Dominions, successfully asserted at the Peace Conference, had to wait till 1926 for its full recognition at an Imperial Conference and till 1931 for its legal confirmation by the Statute of

[1] Neville Chamberlain and his half-brother Austen were both sons of Joseph Chamberlain.

Westminster; the Dominions Office had already in 1925 been separated from the Colonial Office. The acceptance of Dominion self-determination made possible a settlement of the Irish question in 1921. It satisfied neither Irish nationalism nor unbending Toryism, but it brought an end to civil war in Ireland, secured the six Protestant counties and gave a respite for normal relations to grow up between the peoples of the two islands. In 1937, however, the new constitution of "Eire" eliminated the Crown for all internal purposes. The idea of Dominion status played its part also in modifying the British attitude to Indian aspirations. In 1935, after years of civil disturbance in India and stubborn controversy at home, the National government passed an Act going far beyond that of 1919 and envisaging an all-Indian federation based on responsible government, except for certain "safeguards," both in the Provinces and at the centre; unfortunately, by the end of our period only the part concerning the Provinces could be brought into operation.

In the dependent Empire, as it came to be known, outside India, the principle of the Dual Mandate, namely the responsibility of the dominant power both for the welfare of the native peoples and for making available the natural resources of the country to the outside world, was generally recognized. With reference to

Kenya, where Europeans and Indians had super-
imposed themselves upon the vast African
majority, the British government recorded in
1923 "their considered opinion that the interests
of the African natives must be paramount,
and that if and when those interests and the
interests of the immigrant races should conflict,
the former should prevail." But it would be
rash to claim that this principle was invariably
respected.

In the Middle East, the Mandate for Iraq was
surrendered in exchange for a treaty in 1922,
but it proved impossible to govern the mandated
territory of Palestine in such a way as to satisfy
the just aspirations of both Arabs and Jews, and
towards the end of the period there was constant
trouble. Egypt, over which a British pro-
tectorate had been proclaimed in the war, was
declared a sovereign independent state; the
quarrel with the nationalists continued, however,
until 1936, when under the shadow of Italian
expansionism a treaty was signed restricting
British troops to the Canal Zone and providing
for joint Anglo-Egyptian control in the Sudan
and for an alliance in the event of war.

The extension of self-government to the
Dominions was not accompanied, as was hoped
in London, by a parallel consolidation of the
Imperial tie and the establishment of appropriate

R

institutions, such as an Imperial secretariat or Appeal Court. Anything of the sort was repugnant to Canadian and South African, much less so to Australian and New Zealand, nationalism. The diplomatic unity of the Empire was once for all abandoned in 1925, when the Dominions stood out from the all-important Locarno treaties; and when the United Kingdom went to war with Germany in 1939 it was by no means certain that all of them would follow suit, though in fact all did, except Eire, which remained neutral.

In foreign as well as home affairs there was disillusionment. The British people welcomed the League of Nations, if with varying degrees of enthusiasm and confidence, and were determined at least to give it a fair trial. Planned in accordance with Anglo-American ideas, the League was an adaptation of the nineteenth-century system of a Concert of Europe and occasional international conferences to the wider world of the twentieth, with a permanent organization and home at Geneva. Member states were pledged to submit disputes to peaceful discussion before resorting to war, to restrain by joint action states which broke this pledge, to reduce their armaments, and to take into consideration international engagements and conditions generally whose continuance might endanger peace. Some of the most important articles of the Covenant were loosely phrased and its obligations could be variously interpreted. This proved to be especially the case with regard to the principle of "collective security"—a subject on which emotion and hard thinking did not always go together.

The League depended for success on the collaboration of the United States, the United Kingdom and France. In fact, the United States never joined, thereby upsetting the balance, and shattering the confidence of the weaker powers. Left to themselves France and Britain failed to work together or give the necessary lead. The French resented as a betrayal the British withdrawal from the projected guarantee of French security to which the United States and the United Kingdom were to have been parties; the British disapproved the harsh French attitude to Germany which culminated in the ruinous occupation of the Ruhr district in 1923. In the prevailing atmosphere of passionate anti-militarism and distrust of France no British government could have given France such a promise of automatic and powerful immediate support as alone might have relieved her from the haunting fear of invasion by a revived Germany increasingly superior in numbers and unchanged in heart. Failing such a guarantee the French sought to find security in an extension and strengthening of the provisions of the Covenant and in a system of alliances intended to contain Germany in the east. British opinion, and still more that of the Dominions, was suspicious of any extension of the obligations of the Covenant, disliking automatic commitments, and the Geneva Protocol, to which the Labour government had given its approval in 1924, was rejected by the Conservatives. But hopes were restored by the conclusion in 1925, by the joint efforts of Austen Chamberlain, Stresemann and Briand, of the Locarno agreements placing the frontier between France, Belgium and Germany under the guarantee of Britain and Italy; next year Germany was admitted to the League and a brighter day seemed to have dawned. Still better, as optimists believed, in 1928 American initiative resulted in the universal abjuration, by the Paris Pact, of war "as an instrument of national policy;" but there was no provision for enforcement.

The acid test of peaceful intentions was disarmament, and in this matter weary years of negotiation, in which Lord Robert Cecil played a conspicuous and devoted part, brought no success. The principal naval powers had indeed consented at Washington in 1922 to scale down their capital ships to a fixed ratio, and they agreed

to build no new ones till 1936; an agreement as
to cruisers was reached later, after acrimonious
discussions, between Britain and the United
States.   On land and in the air Britain had after
the armistice reduced her immense forces to tiny
proportions, the government having decided that
no major war need be apprehended for ten
years—a decision which ruled until 1932.   Not
till 1934–5 was rearmament taken in hand, and
then on a very modest scale.   It was with regard
to the land and air forces of the Continental
powers that the difficulty and danger lay.   The
Germans, as their prosperity and morale revived,
claimed equal status with other powers, and
this was just what, in the matter of armaments,
the French would not concede, or would concede
only after a period of probation.   British
diplomacy worked hard to bring the two together
but without success.   In 1933 Germany finally
left the League as well as the Disarmament
Conference, proceeding in 1935 to form a large
conscript army in open defiance of the Treaty of
Versailles.

Economic and moral exhaustion, popular
revulsion from the thought of war and prolonged
hopes of general disarmament explain the failure
of successive British governments to safeguard
the nation's security in the face of mounting
threats from militaristic powers.   Japan started

on the path of aggression in 1931, occupying Manchuria and flouting Western interests in China; to what extent the British Foreign Office missed an opportunity of American co-operation in checking her remains controversial. In Germany parliamentary government broke down in 1932, and next year the National Socialists, under Adolf Hitler, assumed power, instituting a regime of brutality at home and aggression abroad; the decision to create a large army and air force, the remilitarization of the Rhineland contrary to the Locarno agreements, intervention in the Spanish civil war, the annexations of Austria and the Sudeten districts of Czechoslovakia were the milestones in their march, to be followed in 1939 by the incorporation of the remaining Czech lands and the invasion of Poland.

The same reasons, along with a widespread feeling that Germany had been hardly treated and the knowledge of our own military weakness and a similar lack of strong leadership in France, explain the failure of the Baldwin and Chamberlain governments to call a halt to Germany's aggression while it was still possible to do this without war. The last chance was lost when Hitler marched a token force into the Rhineland in March 1936, but the feeling of the country was strongly against intervention, even had not the greater part of our small available forces been away in the Mediterranean.

Italian democracy had succumbed as early as 1921 to the ambitious militarism of Mussolini and his blackshirts. This ex-Socialist dictator was ready at first to form part of a common front against the dictator north of the Alps, but in 1935 his designs against Abyssinia brought him up against the League. The Baldwin government had at the recent general election pledged its full support to the League, and felt bound to take the lead in organizing economic sanctions against Italy; but their determination not to go to the length of war—which was shared by the other members—involved both the League and their country in a humiliating defeat. The British attitude was largely influenced by that of France, who, obsessed by the German danger, was resolved not to provoke Italy unduly. Henceforward "collective security" was dead, and the two dictators, along with Japan, soon bound themselves together in opposition ostensibly to Communism but in fact also to the satisfied powers of the West. The possibility of the simultaneous hostility of three powers was something we had never prepared against, and one which our diminished navy was incapable of meeting. The only hope was that if the Japanese made war on us we should have the

United States as our ally. But America was now firmly isolationist.

Throughout the period Russia remained an enigma. Her fundamental dislike of the Western "capitalistic" powers, which had supported the anti-revolutionary forces in 1919, was obvious, but it was not clear whether this need prevent commercial intercourse. British socialists were sentimentally inclined to give the Soviets the benefit of the doubt, and the two Labour governments tried without success to establish friendly relations. Russia, however, like the Western powers was alarmed by the rise of Nazism and in 1934 joined the League. It was the Franco-Russian pact of 1935 which gave Hitler his excuse for tearing up the Locarno treaties. Whether, with more skilful diplomacy on the part of the West, Russian co-operation to restrain Germany could have been achieved must remain a matter of conjecture, for the distrust of Russia felt by most Western statesmen and also by Russia's small neighbours was ineradicable, and when eleventh-hour attempts were made to concert resistance they were foiled by her duplicity. The Nazi-Soviet pact of August 23, 1939, made a European war certain.

All British governments in these twenty years, despite the eloquent warnings of Winston Churchill, were pacific to a fault. What was meant to be the appeasement of Europe turned out to be the appeasement of Germany. Men like Baldwin and Chamberlain, Simon and Halifax did not understand the gangster mentality: they believed they could do business with Hitler, whereas we now know that he was all along resolved to enlarge Germany's "living space" to the east, if necessary by war. Opinions will long differ whether things would have worked out better if in September 1938 the British and French governments, faced by Hitler's imminent aggression against the Czechs, had declared war instead of counselling the Czechs to sacrifice large parts of their country. Neither side was then as ready for war as in 1939—the British, one should rather say, were even more unready—and one can only guess what would have happened if Chamberlain had not taken his historic flights to meet Hitler and brought back from Munich what he wrongly believed to be the assurance of Anglo-German amity. Certainly the people of the United Kingdom, and still more those of the Dominions, would have been deeply divided as to whether war was at that time justified or expedient. But when Hitler in the following March wantonly broke up the Czechoslovak state by force the whole country, including the Prime Minister, was converted to the necessity of resistance if Germany

s

was not to destroy the liberties of the world. Rearmament was speeded up, conscription was enacted and guarantees of automatic help were rashly and, as it proved, ineffectually given to Poland, Greece and Roumania. The invasion of Poland on 1st September brought the first of these guarantees into effect and within a few days France and the British Empire were again at war with Germany.

It had been generally expected that war would begin with a full-scale bombing of London— the nightmare of many years—and elaborate schemes had been drawn up to meet the threat by the evacuation of children and the construction of shelters as well as by active defence measures. The Germans, however, had no such attack in mind as yet. Except at sea, where the Navy was always at full stretch, eight months of comparative quiet gave the country a needed respite to prepare for another long war.

TABLE OF MINISTRIES, 1815–1918

Date	Prime Minister	Foreign Secretary	Party
June 1812	Earl of Liverpool	Viscount Castlereagh	T.
April 1827	G. Canning	G. Canning (1822) Viscount Dudley	,,
	Viscount Goderich (Sept., 1827)	,, ,,	
Jan. 1828	Duke of Wellington	Earl of Aberdeen (May, 1828)	
Nov. 1830	Earl Grey	Viscount Palmerston	W.
	Viscount Melbourne (1834)		
Dec. 1834	Sir R. Peel	Duke of Wellington	C.
April 1835	Viscount Melbourne	Viscount Palmerston	W.
Sept. 1841	Sir R. Peel	Earl of Aberdeen	C.
July 1846	Lord J. Russell	Viscount Palmerston	W.
		Earl Granville (1851)	
Feb. 1852	Earl of Derby	Earl of Malmesbury	C.
Dec. 1852	Earl of Aberdeen	Lord J. Russell	Coal.
		Earl of Clarendon (1853)	
Feb. 1855	Viscount Palmerston		W.
Feb. 1858	Earl of Derby	Earl of Malmesbury	C.
June 1859	Viscount Palmerston	Lord J. Russell (Earl Russell)	W.-L.
		Earl of Clarendon	
July 1866	Earl of Derby	Lord Stanley	C.
	B. Disraeli (1868)	,, ,, (Earl of Derby)	
Dec. 1868	W. E. Gladstone	Earl of Clarendon	L.
		Earl Granville (1870)	
Feb. 1874	B. Disraeli (Earl of Beaconsfield)	Earl of Derby	C.
		Marquis of Salisbury (1878)	
April 1880	W. E. Gladstone	Earl Granville	L.
June 1885	Marquis of Salisbury	Marquis of Salisbury	C.
Feb. 1886	W. E. Gladstone	Earl of Rosebery	L.
Aug. 1886	Marquis of Salisbury	Earl of Iddesleigh	C.
		Marquis of Salisbury (1887)	
Aug. 1892	W. E. Gladstone	Earl of Rosebery	L.
	Earl of Rosebery (1894)	Earl of Kimberley (1894)	
July 1895	Marquis of Salisbury	Marquis of Salisbury	U.
	A. J. Balfour (1902)	Marquis of Lansdowne (1900)	
Dec. 1905	Sir H. Campbell-Bannerman	Sir E. Grey	L.
	H. H. Asquith (1908)	,, ,,	
June 1915			Coal.
Dec. 1916	D. Lloyd George	A. J. Balfour	,,

T. = Tory ; W. = Whig ; C. = Conservative ; Coal. = Coalition ; L. = Liberal ; U. = Unionist.

TABLE OF MINISTRIES—(*continued*)
1919–39

Date	Prime Minister	Foreign Secretary	Party
1919	D. Lloyd George	A. J. Balfour	Coal.
		Marquis Curzon (Oct.)	,,
Oct. 1922	A. Bonar Law	,, ,,	C.
May 1923	S. Baldwin	,, ,,	,,
Jan. 1924	J. R. MacDonald	J. R. MacDonald	Lab.
Nov. 1924	S. Baldwin	A. Chamberlain	C.
June 1929	J. R. MacDonald	A. Henderson	Lab.
Aug. 1931	,, ,,	Marquis of Reading	Nat.
Nov. 1931	,, ,,	Sir J. Simon	,,
June 1935	S. Baldwin	Sir S. Hoare	,,
		A. Eden (Dec.)	,,
May 1937	N. Chamberlain		,,
		Viscount Halifax (Feb. 1938)	,,

Coal. = Coalition; C. = Conservative; Lab. = Labour;
Nat. = National.

BIBLIOGRAPHICAL NOTE

(*Revised* 1959)

The best general history for the periods which it covers is Halévy, *A History of the English People* (6 vols., translated, covering 1815–52 and 1895–1915). The whole period up to 1914 is now treated in two volumes of the *Oxford History of England*: Woodward, *The Age of Reform*, and Ensor, *England 1870–1914*. The best short history of the war of 1914–18 is Cruttwell's *History of the Great War*. There is no comparable work for the period after 1918, but it is covered by C. L. Mowat's *Britain between the Two Wars*. The 4 vols. of the *History of "The Times"* are of interest for the whole period, and a narrative of events, year by year, is given in the *Annual Register*.

Among contemporary sources for the nineteenth century, *The Greville Memoirs* (ed. Strachey and Fulford, 8 vols.) and Queen Victoria's *Letters* (9 vols.) are of special interest on the political side. For the twentieth century the following may be mentioned: L. S. Amery, *My Political Life*; Beaverbrook, *Politicians and the War*; Churchill, *The Second World War* (vol. 1, *The Gathering Storm*, 2nd and later edns.); Dalton, *Call Back Yesterday* and *The Fateful Years*; Lloyd George, *War Memoirs* and *The Truth about the Peace Treaties*; Percy, *Some Memories*; Templewood (Sir Samuel Hoare), *Nine Troubled Years*; Norwich (Duff Cooper), *Old Men Forget*.

Among biographies of public persons the following may be mentioned: Lord Grey of the Reform Bill, by

G. M. Trevelyan; Macaulay, by Sir G. O. Trevelyan; Gladstone, by Morley, and by Magnus; Cobden, by Morley; Bright, by G. M. Trevelyan; Disraeli, by Monypenny and Buckle; Salisbury, by Lady G. Cecil (to 1892); Lord Randolph Churchill, by Winston Churchill, also by R. R. James; Joseph Chamberlain, by Garvin and J. Amery (4 vols. so far, to 1903); Campbell-Bannerman, by Spender; Asquith, by Spender and Cyril Asquith; Balfour, by Dugdale; Bonar Law (*The Unknown Prime Minister*), by Blake; Baldwin (*My Father, the true story*), by A. W. Baldwin; Neville Chamberlain, by Feiling; Henderson, by M. A. Hamilton; Montagu Norman, by Clay; Keynes, by Harrod; King George V, by Nicolson; Archbishop Davidson, by Bell; Archbishop Lang, by Lockhart. There are studies of Queen Victoria by Strachey, of Brougham by Aspinall, of Peel by Rosebery and by Kitson Clark, of Palmerston by Guedalla.

On the constitutional and administrative sides the standard works are Erskine May (3 vols., ed. Holland); Redlich and Hurst, *English Local Government*; and S. and B. Webb's studies in local government. There is much recent history in Jennings' two volumes on *Cabinet* and *Parliament*. See also the monographs by Fulford on *Votes for Women*, by Julian Symon on *The General Strike*, and by R. Bassett, *Nineteen Thirty-one*; *Political Crisis*.

For Ireland, see Hammond, *Gladstone and the Irish Nation*, and Pakenham, *Peace by Ordeal*; for colonial and imperial history, see the *Cambridge History of the British Empire*, vols. ii and iii; Hancock, *Survey of British Commonwealth Affairs* (3 vols.); Lucas, *Lord Durham's Report*; Lugard, *The Dual Mandate*. Among shorter works, Egerton, *Short History of British Colonial Policy*, and Walker, *The British Empire, its Structure and Spirit*, may be mentioned. There is a masterly summary of recent Indian constitutional history in the *Report of the*

Indian Statutory Commission (the "Simon Report"), 1930, vol. 1, Cmd. 3568.

For foreign policy, see Algernon Cecil, *British Foreign Secretaries*; the studies of Castlereagh and Canning by Webster and by Temperley; of Palmerston by Bell and by Webster (to 1841); Hobson's *Richard Cobden, the international man*; on the Crimean War, Simpson, *Louis Napoleon and the Ascendancy of France*, Martin, *The Triumph of Lord Palmerston*, Temperley, *England and the Near East*; on Anglo-American relations, R. B. Mowat, *Diplomatic Relations of Great Britain and the United States*; on the seventies and eighties, the lives of Lyons by Newton and of Granville by Fitzmaurice; on the period after 1890, Grey, *Twenty-five Years*; Brandenburg, *From Bismarck to the World War*; Spender, *Fifty Years of Europe*; Albertini, *Origins of the War of 1914* (translated); Nicolson, *Lord Carnock, Peacemaking 1919*, and *Curzon, the past Phase*; Viscount Cecil, *A Great Experiment*; Seton-Watson, *Britain and the Dictators*; Jordan, *Great Britain, France, and the German Problem, 1918–39*.

On the economic side the standard work is Clapham, *Economic History of Modern Britain* (3 vols.); on a smaller scale are Knowles, *Industrial and Commercial Revolutions*; Fay, *Great Britain from Adam Smith to the Present Day*; Court, *Concise Economic History of Britain*; and Jones and Pool, *A Hundred Years of Economic Development*; Porter, *Progress of the Nation* (ed. Hirst), is a mine of statistics. Social conditions in the period before 1832, as they affected the poor, are brilliantly described by J. L. and B. Hammond in their trilogy *The Village Labourer*, *The Town Labourer* and *The Skilled Labourer*, and also, more summarily, in their *Rise of Modern Industry*. Their conclusions should be compared with those arrived at by Clapham and by Gonner, *Common Land and Inclosure*. For agriculture, see Ernle, *English Farming*,

Past and Present. Other special subjects are treated by Griffith, *Population Problems of the Age of Malthus*; Redford, *Labour Migration in England 1800–50*; Engels, *Condition of the Working Classes in England in 1844*; Hutchins and Harrison, *History of Factory Legislation*; Hovell, *The Chartist Movement*; Potter, *The Co-operative Movement in Great Britain*; Webb, *History of Trade Unionism*; Cole, *Short History of the British Working Class Movement*; Layton and Crowther, *Introduction to the Study of Prices.* The British Association Reports, *Britain in Recovery* and *Britain in Depression,* may be consulted. Cobbett's *Rural Rides,* W. Lovett's *Life and Struggles,* and the lives of Francis Place by Wallas, Cobbett and Owen by Cole, and Shaftesbury by J. L. and B. Hammond should also be mentioned.

Among books throwing light on the history of thought are Hazlitt, *Spirit of the Age* (1825); Coleridge, *Table Talk* (1835); Dicey, *Law and Public Opinion in England*; L. Stephen, *The English Utilitarians*; Beer, *History of British Socialism*; Church, *The Oxford Movement*; Newman, *Apologia pro Vita Sua*; Stanley, *Life of Arnold*; Raven, *Christian Socialism*; Darwin, *Origin of Species*; J. S. Mill, *Autobiography*; M. Arnold, *Culture and Anarchy*; Mackail, *Life of William Morris*; Morley, *Recollections*; B. Stephen, *Emily Davies and Girton College*; B. Webb, *My Apprenticeship* and *Our Partnership*; Whitehead, *Science and the Modern World,* chaps. v, vi.

INDEX

PRINTED IN
GREAT BRITAIN
BY
THE RIVERSIDE PRESS
EDINBURGH